GOOD WOOD
JOINTS

GOOD WOOD
JOINTS

Albert Jackson & David Day

BETTERWAY BOOKS
CINCINNATI, OHIO

GOOD WOOD JOINTS
Conceived, edited and designed at Inklink,
Greenwich, London, England

Text: Albert Jackson and David Day
Design and art direction: Simon Jennings

Text editors: Ian Kearey
and Albert Jackson

Illustrators: Robin Harris and David Day

Examples of joints: William Brooker

Studio photography: Paul Chave, Ben Jennings
and Neil Waving

Indexer: Ian Kearey

U.S. consultant editor: R. Adam Blake

Technical consultant: John Perkins

First published in North America
in 1995 by Betterway Books,
an imprint of F & W Publications, Inc.
1507 Dana Avenue
Cincinnati, OH 45207
1–800/289–0963

ISBN 1–55870–408–6

Text set in Franklin Gothic Extra Condensed, Univers Condensed
and Garamond Book Condensed by Inklink, London

Printed in Singapore

Jacket design: Simon Jennings
Jacket photographs: Paul Chave
Jacket illustrations: Robin Harris and David Day

ACKNOWLEDGEMENTS

The authors would like to thank the following for the supply of reference
material and equipment used in the production of this book.

Kenneth Grisley,
Leigh Industries Ltd,
Port Coquitlam, BC,
Canada

Jim Pankhania,
Elu Power Tools Ltd,
Slough, Berks, UK
(also for the photograph on page 91)

Ramon Weston,
Leigh Industries (UK) Ltd,
Chippenham, Wilts, UK

Jim Phillips,
Trend Machinery and Cutting Tools,
Watford, Herts, UK

CONTENTS

INTRODUCTION	6
FIRST PRINCIPLES	9
SELECTING THE RIGHT JOINT	10
BASIC ESSENTIALS	14
WORKSHOP SAFETY	16
BUTT JOINTS	17
EDGE-TO-EDGE JOINTS	25
DOWEL JOINTS	29
BRIDLE JOINTS	35
RABBET JOINTS	41
DADO JOINTS	47
HALF-LAP JOINTS	55
MORTISE-AND-TENON JOINTS	63
DOVETAIL JOINTS	81
FINGER JOINTS	95
HINGE JOINTS	99
KNOCK-DOWN JOINTS	105
TOOLS AND MACHINES	111
CLAMPING JOINTS	124
ADHESIVES	126

INTRODUCTION

What is a cabinet-maker, if not a skilled maker of joints? The colour of the wood, or perhaps a near-perfect surface finish, may be the initial things that draw our attention to a piece of work, but it isn't very long before we slide open a drawer or begin peering inside a cupboard to see and feel the quality of the joints. This is hardly surprising, because many people consider joint-making to be the true measure of a crafts-man, not least because cutting fine joints requires in-depth knowledge of one's materials and a degree of proficiency with a wide variety of handtools or machines. In addition, there is the choice of joint, which reveals something about a wood-worker's level of experience. A joint must, first of all, be functional to provide sufficient strength, but it should also be in keeping with the overall style of the piece for which it is intended – in short, it must be the right joint for the job.

CHAPTER 1

This book does not set out to be a manual on woodworking. It assumes that you are familiar with the basics, yet want to know more about which joints you can use to achieve your goal and how best to make them. The book also aims to provide you with a variety of options, suggesting a number of different joints that you could choose for a specific purpose and, where appropriate, alternative methods for cutting those joints with handtools, power tools and woodworking machines.

FIRST PRINCIPLES

SELECTING THE RIGHT JOINT

Before you can exercise your woodworking skills, you have to decide which joint will best suit your needs; given that there are so many to choose from, making the right choice is not as easy at it might seem. These charts suggest not only which joints to consider for a wide variety of applications, but also what tools you can use and what materials will be suitable.

Finding recommended joints

From the diagrams ranged along the top of the charts, select the application that most closely represents the item you want to make. For example, do you want to join chair legs to a seat rail, or the corners of a cabinet, or do you want to know what joints to use for constructing frames or drawers? Having found the diagram that includes the type of joint you need, match the numbers below it with those found in the top left-hand corner of recommended joints illustrated in the chart.

Ease of making

Each illustration also includes a colour box that indicates whether it is possible to make that particular joint with handtools or machine tools. The letter on the colour box indicates whether it is relatively easy (**E**) or difficult (**D**) to make with those tools (see key below).

Hand tools	Machine tools
E *Easy*	**E** *Easy*
D *Difficult*	**D** *Difficult*

Materials and suitability

The number-rated colour banding below each illustration is designed to help you decide whether the joint is suitable for the material you are intending to use. Thus, a red box containing number **2** indicates that the joint will be good for solid-wood construction (see key below).

Material	colour code	Suitability
Solid wood		**1** *Excellent*
Plywood		**2** *Good*
Blockboard		**3** *Fair*
Chipboard		**4** *Poor*
MDF		

Page references

Finally, the numbers in the top right-hand corner of each illustration refer you to the page or pages where the construction of each joint is described in full.

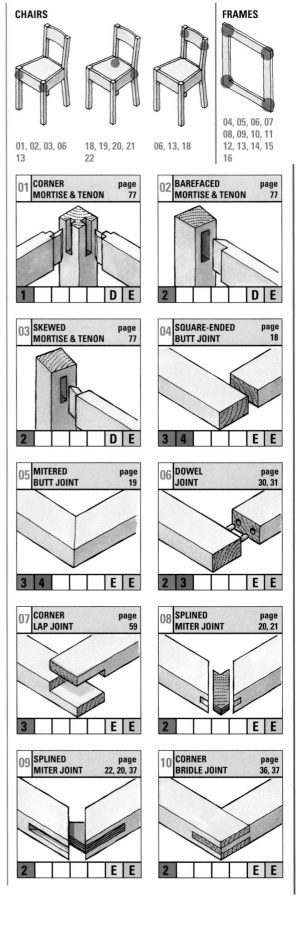

CHAIRS

01, 02, 03, 06 13

18, 19, 20, 21 22

06, 13, 18

FRAMES

04, 05, 06, 07
08, 09, 10, 11
12, 13, 14, 15
16

01 CORNER MORTISE & TENON — page 77
1 D E

02 BAREFACED MORTISE & TENON — page 77
2 D E

03 SKEWED MORTISE & TENON — page 77
2 D E

04 SQUARE-ENDED BUTT JOINT — page 18
3 4 E E

05 MITERED BUTT JOINT — page 19
3 4 E E

06 DOWEL JOINT — page 30, 31
2 3 E E

07 CORNER LAP JOINT — page 59
3 E E

08 SPLINED MITER JOINT — page 20, 21
2 E E

09 SPLINED MITER JOINT — page 22, 20, 37
2 E E

10 CORNER BRIDLE JOINT — page 36, 37
2 E E

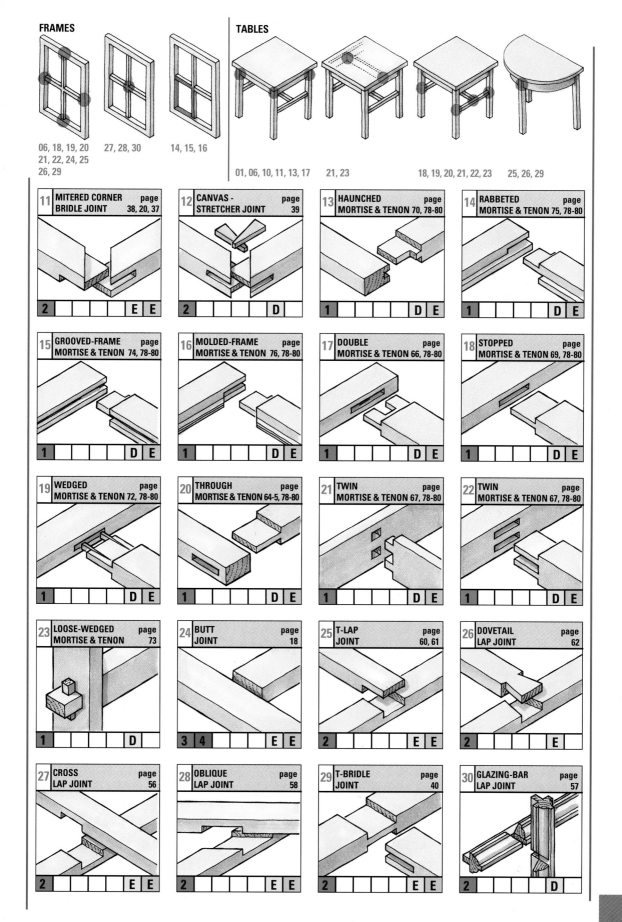

06, 18, 19, 20
21, 22, 24, 25
26, 29

27, 28, 30

14, 15, 16

01, 06, 10, 11, 13, 17   21, 23   18, 19, 20, 21, 22, 23   25, 26, 29

11 MITERED CORNER BRIDLE JOINT — page 38, 20, 37 — `2` E E

12 CANVAS - STRETCHER JOINT — page 39 — `2` D

13 HAUNCHED MORTISE & TENON — page 70, 78-80 — `1` D E

14 RABBETED MORTISE & TENON — page 75, 78-80 — `1` D E

15 GROOVED-FRAME MORTISE & TENON — page 74, 78-80 — `1` D E

16 MOLDED-FRAME MORTISE & TENON — page 76, 78-80 — `1` D E

17 DOUBLE MORTISE & TENON — page 66, 78-80 — `1` D E

18 STOPPED MORTISE & TENON — page 69, 78-80 — `1` D E

19 WEDGED MORTISE & TENON — page 72, 78-80 — `1` D E

20 THROUGH MORTISE & TENON — page 64-5, 78-80 — `1` D E

21 TWIN MORTISE & TENON — page 67, 78-80 — `1` D E

22 TWIN MORTISE & TENON — page 67, 78-80 — `1` D E

23 LOOSE-WEDGED MORTISE & TENON — page 73 — `1` D

24 BUTT JOINT — page 18 — `3` `4` E E

25 T-LAP JOINT — page 60, 61 — `2` E E

26 DOVETAIL LAP JOINT — page 62 — `2` E

27 CROSS LAP JOINT — page 56 — `2` E E

28 OBLIQUE LAP JOINT — page 58 — `2` E E

29 T-BRIDLE JOINT — page 40 — `2` E E

30 GLAZING-BAR LAP JOINT — page 57 — `2` D

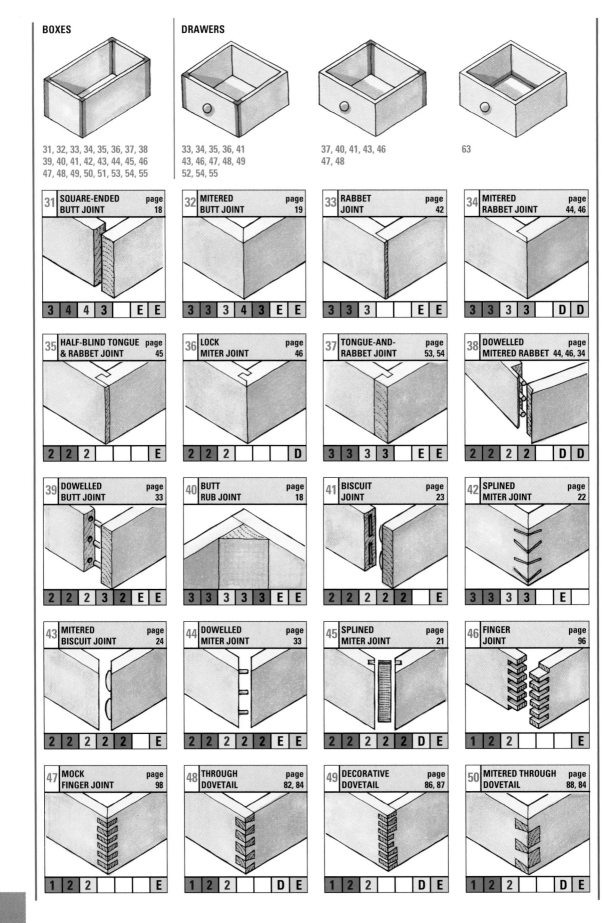

BOXES

31, 32, 33, 34, 35, 36, 37, 38
39, 40, 41, 42, 43, 44, 45, 46
47, 48, 49, 50, 51, 53, 54, 55

DRAWERS

33, 34, 35, 36, 41
43, 46, 47, 48, 49
52, 54, 55

37, 40, 41, 43, 46
47, 48

63

| 31 | SQUARE-ENDED BUTT JOINT | page 18 |
| 3 | 4 | 4 | 3 | | E | E |

| 32 | MITERED BUTT JOINT | page 19 |
| 3 | 3 | 3 | 4 | 3 | E | E |

| 33 | RABBET JOINT | page 42 |
| 3 | 3 | 3 | | | E | E |

| 34 | MITERED RABBET JOINT | page 44, 46 |
| 3 | 3 | 3 | 3 | | D | D |

| 35 | HALF-BLIND TONGUE & RABBET JOINT | page 45 |
| 2 | 2 | 2 | | | | E |

| 36 | LOCK MITER JOINT | page 46 |
| 2 | 2 | 2 | | | | D |

| 37 | TONGUE-AND-RABBET JOINT | page 53, 54 |
| 3 | 3 | 3 | 3 | | E | E |

| 38 | DOWELLED MITERED RABBET | page 44, 46, 34 |
| 2 | 2 | 2 | 2 | | D | D |

| 39 | DOWELLED BUTT JOINT | page 33 |
| 2 | 2 | 2 | 3 | 2 | E | E |

| 40 | BUTT RUB JOINT | page 18 |
| 3 | 3 | 3 | 3 | 3 | E | E |

| 41 | BISCUIT JOINT | page 23 |
| 2 | 2 | 2 | 2 | 2 | | E |

| 42 | SPLINED MITER JOINT | page 22 |
| 3 | 3 | 3 | | | E | |

| 43 | MITERED BISCUIT JOINT | page 24 |
| 2 | 2 | 2 | 2 | 2 | | E |

| 44 | DOWELLED MITER JOINT | page 33 |
| 2 | 2 | 2 | 2 | 2 | E | E |

| 45 | SPLINED MITER JOINT | page 21 |
| 2 | 2 | 2 | 2 | 2 | D | E |

| 46 | FINGER JOINT | page 96 |
| 1 | 2 | 2 | | | | E |

| 47 | MOCK FINGER JOINT | page 98 |
| 1 | 2 | 2 | | | | E |

| 48 | THROUGH DOVETAIL | page 82, 84 |
| 1 | 2 | 2 | | | D | E |

| 49 | DECORATIVE DOVETAIL | page 86, 87 |
| 1 | 2 | 2 | | | D | E |

| 50 | MITERED THROUGH DOVETAIL | page 88, 84 |
| 1 | 2 | 2 | | | D | E |

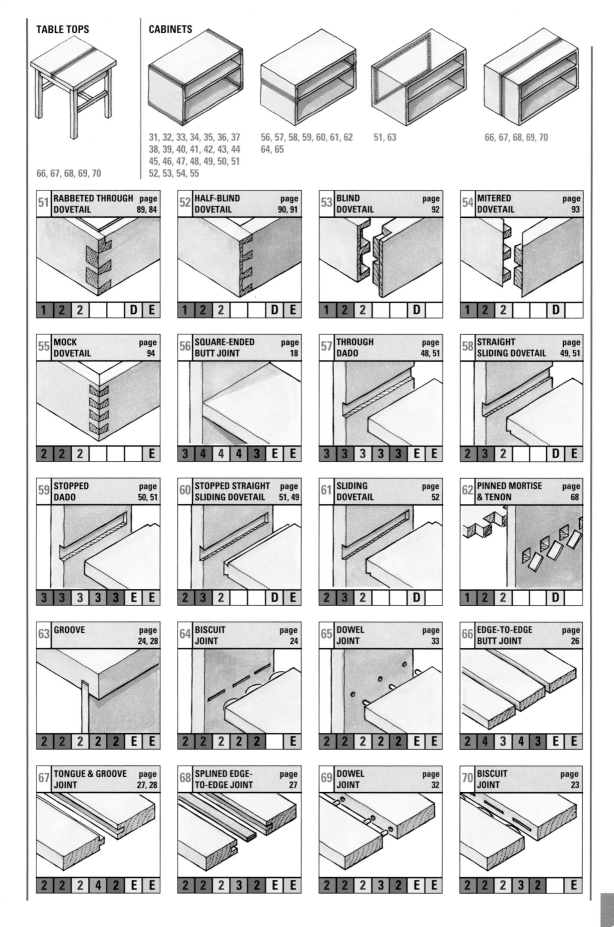

TABLE TOPS

66, 67, 68, 69, 70

CABINETS

31, 32, 33, 34, 35, 36, 37
38, 39, 40, 41, 42, 43, 44
45, 46, 47, 48, 49, 50, 51
52, 53, 54, 55

56, 57, 58, 59, 60, 61, 62
64, 65

51, 63

66, 67, 68, 69, 70

51	RABBETED THROUGH DOVETAIL	page 89, 84
52	HALF-BLIND DOVETAIL	page 90, 91
53	BLIND DOVETAIL	page 92
54	MITERED DOVETAIL	page 93

51: 1 2 2 D E
52: 1 2 2 D E
53: 1 2 2 D
54: 1 2 2 D

55	MOCK DOVETAIL	page 94
56	SQUARE-ENDED BUTT JOINT	page 18
57	THROUGH DADO	page 48, 51
58	STRAIGHT SLIDING DOVETAIL	page 49, 51

55: 2 2 2 E
56: 3 4 4 4 3 E E
57: 3 3 3 3 3 E E
58: 2 3 2 D E

59	STOPPED DADO	page 50, 51
60	STOPPED STRAIGHT SLIDING DOVETAIL	page 51, 49
61	SLIDING DOVETAIL	page 52
62	PINNED MORTISE & TENON	page 68

59: 3 3 3 3 3 E E
60: 2 3 2 D E
61: 2 3 2 D
62: 1 2 2 D

63	GROOVE	page 24, 28
64	BISCUIT JOINT	page 24
65	DOWEL JOINT	page 33
66	EDGE-TO-EDGE BUTT JOINT	page 26

63: 2 2 2 2 2 E E
64: 2 2 2 2 2 E
65: 2 2 2 2 2 E E
66: 2 4 3 4 3 E E

67	TONGUE & GROOVE JOINT	page 27, 28
68	SPLINED EDGE-TO-EDGE JOINT	page 27
69	DOWEL JOINT	page 32
70	BISCUIT JOINT	page 23

67: 2 2 2 4 2 E E
68: 2 2 2 3 2 E E
69: 2 2 2 3 2 E E
70: 2 2 2 3 2 E

13

BASIC ESSENTIALS

As with most craft skills, there is hardly ever only one way to cut a joint. With experience, every woodworker adapts the basic methods, incorporating small personal variations that make the job easier or produce a better result for them. Nevertheless, there is a hard core of accepted procedures and techniques that are consistent with snug-fitting joints.

Accurate marking-out

The old adage, 'measure twice and cut once', is good advice. Hurried, inaccurate work when marking out joints leads to all manner of problems. Buy well-made rules and tape measures, and always stick to either the imperial or metric systems of measurement – the conversions quoted in this book are approximate only. Mark out overall dimensions with a sharp pencil, but use a marking knife to score lines that are to be cut, so as to avoid leaving a rough edge of torn wood fibers. Always run the flat face of the knife against the try square or straightedge. Use a sharp pencil to emphasize a knifed line that is difficult to see; on dark-coloured woods, rub the surface with white chalk to accentuate the line.

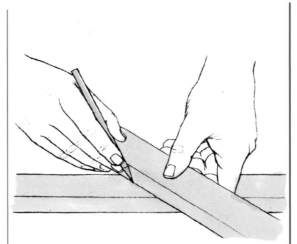

Marking one component from another

Whenever possible, mark one component from another, rather than relying on measurements.

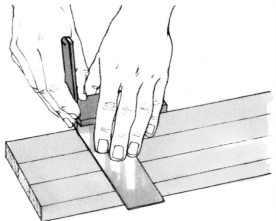

Marking identical components

If an assembly includes several identical components, lay them together on the bench and mark them out at the same time.

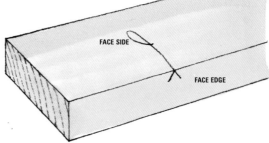

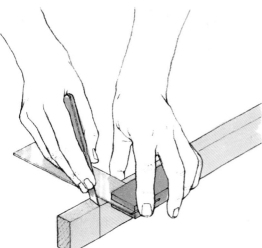

Extending knifed lines

When cutting shoulder lines all round a piece of wood, locate the point of the knife in the cut you have just made, then slide the try square up against the blade.

Squaring timber

When preparing timber for jointing, plane two adjoining surfaces perfectly square, taking all subsequent measurements and angles from them. Conventional symbols are used to denote these surfaces as face side and face edge.

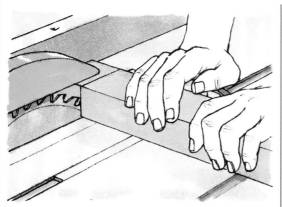

Cutting on the waste side
Allow for the width of a saw cut (the kerf) by always cutting on the waste side of any marked line.

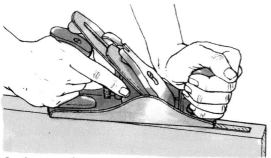

Making a dry assembly
Some professionals claim to be able to glue up an assembly without ever having to check that the joints fit. More cautious woodworkers want to be sure that the shoulders meet snugly, and that they won't have to force a tight joint and risk splitting the wood. Identify each joint with pencil marks so that there is no confusion when it comes to gluing the assembly.

Cutting oversize
When making certain joints, it is good practice to deliberately leave specific elements oversize so that they can be planed flush once the glue has set – the end of a through tenon, for example, or the tips of through dovetails and finger joints.

SELECTING WOOD AND BOARDS
Poorly seasoned, substandard wood adversely affects the strength of a joint. Reject any timber with large knots, splits or other blemishes, and examine your chosen timber carefully, to ensure that there will be no weak short grain at the critical parts of a joint.

Avoid the following blemishes:
1 Large or dead knots
2 Growth-ring shakes
3 End splits
4 Surface checking
5 Honeycomb checks

Don't buy warped or twisted lengths of wood, and check with your supplier that the timber has been seasoned carefully. If it shrinks at a later stage, joints can work loose, and high moisture content may prevent glue setting properly.

Hardwoods
These are generally preferable for finely cut joints; however, provided you make the joints proportionally larger, there is no reason why you shouldn't use good-quality softwoods.

Man-made boards
As a rule, man-made boards do not suffer from the same defects as solid wood, but since most boards lack any real long-grain strength, they are not suitable for the more complex joints (see pages 10-13). In addition, reject any board with a soft crumbly core.

SAFETY IN THE WORKSHOP

Follow basic safety procedures to avoid accidents in the workshop. Blunt tools that you have to force through the wood are potentially more dangerous than sharp ones that cut effortlessly. Always keep your tools and machinery in good condition, checking that spanners and adjusting keys are removed from machines before switching on. Periodically check that all nuts, bolts and other fixings are properly tightened.

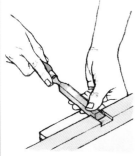

Cutting away from you
For safety, clamp the work or steady it against a bench hook, so that you can keep both hands behind a cutting edge.

OPERATING A MACHINE SAFELY
Make a test cut to check the accuracy of machine settings before cutting an actual workpiece. Either feed the workpiece into the blade, just nicking the edge so that you can check the dimensions, or, for more complicated work, such as a dovetail joint, make a complete test piece out of scrap wood.

Support the work properly when passing it over or through a machine, feeding the work against the direction of rotation of a blade or cutter.

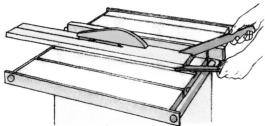

Using a push stick
Use a push stick to feed a workpiece, rather than risking touching a blade with your fingers. Never reach over a blade to remove offcuts.

Guarding blades and cutters
Whenever possible, use proper guards recommended by the machine's manufacturer.
In some of the illustrations in this book, the guards have been omitted for clarity.

Making a temporary guard
If you must remove a fitted guard in order to complete a procedure, make a temporary plywood guard to cover the blade, and attach it to the rip fence. Alternatively, make a sturdy jig that holds the work securely and keeps both hands well away from the blade or cutter.

Changing and adjusting blades
• Don't make adjustments to a machine while cutters or blades are moving, and never slow or stop a blade with a piece of wood; if the machine is not fitted with a brake, switch off and let it come to rest naturally.
• Do not attempt to free a stalled blade or cutter before switching off the machine.
• Disconnect a machine or power tool from the supply of electricity before changing cutters or blades.

PERSONAL CARE
• Tie back long hair, and don't operate a machine or power tool while wearing loose clothing or jewellery that might get caught in moving parts.
• Fit dust extraction to machinery and power tools, or wear a face mask. Use protective eye shields whenever you are doing work which could throw up debris.
• Don't operate a machine under the influence of alcohol or drugs, or if you are feeling drowsy.

WORKSHOP MANAGEMENT
• Don't clutter your bench with tools and pieces of wood. Keep the workshop tidy, and don't let sawdust and shavings build up on the floor – this is a fire hazard and makes the floor slippery.
• Never store materials or equipment above a machine in such a way that they could fall onto it.
• Don't carry a power tool by its cable or use the cable to pull the plug out of a socket. Check the cable and plug regularly for wear or damage.
• Don't throw used batteries from cordless tools into water or a fire, as they are likely to explode.
•After work, disconnect machines and lock your workshop. Keep unsupervised children away from power tools and machinery, even when not in use.

CHAPTER 2 Once you have mastered the skills of cutting and planing wood accurately, assembling butt joints is a simple option for anything from stud partitioning to fine picture framing. Some mitered butt joints will probably be strong enough using glue alone, but it is usually necessary to reinforce square-cut joints in some way.

BUTT JOINTS

SQUARE-ENDED BUTT JOINT
HAND CUT

It is possible to make flat frames and simple box structures utilizing square-cut corner joints. Use sawn timber for rough joinery, but plane the wood square beforehand for good-quality cabinet work. Since glue alone is rarely sufficient to make a sturdy butt joint, hold the parts together with fine finish nails or glued blocks of wood.

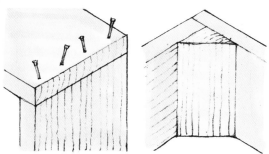

Box-frame joint

Flat-frame joint

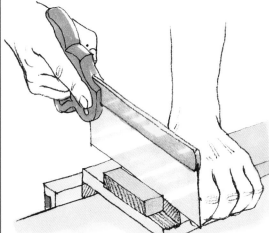

1 Cutting the joint
Mark out each piece of wood to length, using a knife and try square to mark the shoulders of the joint on all faces. Hold the work against a bench hook, and saw down each shoulder, keeping to the waste side of the marked line.

Reinforcing a butt joint
For additional strength, drive nails at an angle into the wood as shown. If you don't want the method of fixing to show on the outside of the joint, glue a corner block on the inside.

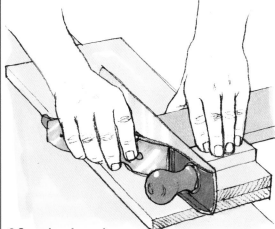

2 Squaring the ends
For all but the most basic work, trim the ends square to form a neat butt joint, using a bench plane and shooting board. Set the plane for a fine cut, and lubricate the running surfaces of the shooting board with a white candle or wax polish.

CUTTING BUTT JOINTS ON A TABLE SAW
A sharp table-saw blade cuts end grain so cleanly that it requires no further finishing. Use a sliding crosscut table or a miter fence to keep the work square to the blade. Set up the machine so that the work can just pass beneath the blade guard.

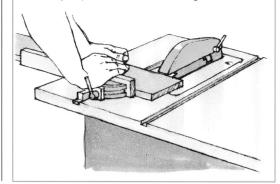

MITERED BUTT JOINT
HAND CUT

The classic joint for picture frames, the mitered butt joint makes a neat right-angle corner without visible end grain. Cutting wood at 45 degrees produces a relatively large surface area of tangentially cut grain that glues well. For lightweight frames, just add glue and set the joint in a miter clamp.

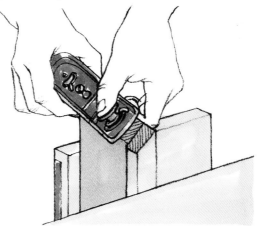

Box-frame miter joint

Flat-frame miter joint

Open joint caused by inaccurate cutting

Inside gap as a result of wood shrinking

Accurate miter cutting

Before you pick up a saw, always ensure that the miter is exactly half the joint angle, or the joint will be gappy. In addition, use well-seasoned timber or a gap may open up on the inside of the joint as the wood shrinks.

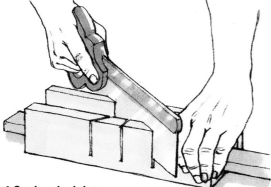

1 Cutting the joint

On each piece of wood, mark the sloping shoulder of the joint, using a knife and miter square. Extend the marked line across the adjacent faces with a try square. To remove the waste, either follow the marked lines by eye or use a miter box to guide the saw blade.

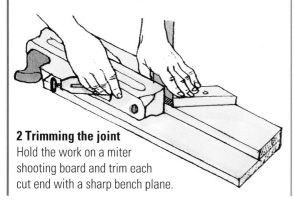

2 Trimming the joint

Hold the work on a miter shooting board and trim each cut end with a sharp bench plane.

Trimming a wide board

Since it is impossible to miter a wide piece of wood on a shooting board, clamp the work upright in a bench vise and trim the end grain with a finely set block plane. To prevent splitting, back up the work with a piece of scrap timber.

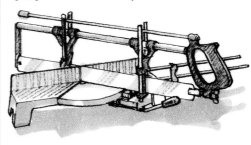

USING A MITER SAW

It pays to use a special jig called a miter saw to cut larger pieces of wood or molded sections of framing. The workpiece can be held on edge or flat on the bed of the tool. The saw guide, which can be set to any angle, guarantees accurate joints.

MITERED BUTT JOINT
MACHINE CUT

Table saws or radial-arm saws make mitering simple, even for compound miters where the angle is in two planes. Reinforcing miter joints with solid wood or plywood splines is also straightforward on a machine; cut the spline slots before gluing machine-made joints. Center the groove in a flat-frame miter, but for a box-frame or cabinet, position the tongue towards the inside of the angle to prevent weak short grain.

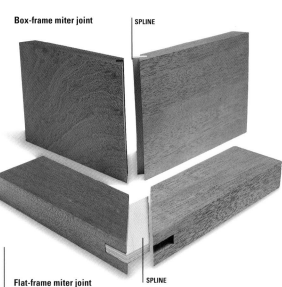

Box-frame miter joint   SPLINE

Flat-frame miter joint   SPLINE

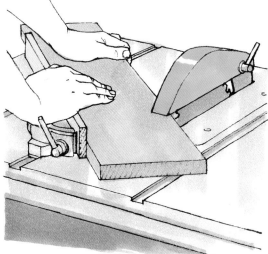

Cutting a flat-frame miter
Adjust the miter fence on the table saw to the required angle, usually 45 degrees. Holding the workpiece firmly against the fence, so that it does not get drawn backwards by the saw, feed it towards the blade.

Cutting a box-frame miter
Tilt the saw blade to 45 degrees to cut a bevel across the board. Set the miter fence at 90 degrees, and feed the work past the blade.

EXTENDING A TABLE-SAW FENCE
The miter fence on most table saws is comparatively short, but some are pre-drilled so that you can screw on a longer hardwood face to extend the fence. Feeding this wooden fence into the saw blade for the first time cuts it perfectly to length. An extended fence not only provides better control, but stops the grain of a workpiece splitting at the back as it is sawn. If you can't fit a permanent extension, sandwich a piece of scrap wood between the fence and the workpiece.

With either method, use both hands to hold the workpiece against the fence, and feed the work quite slowly into the blade. Clamp to the fence any pieces too small to be held with two hands.

A block of wood clamped to the extension serves as a stop for one end of the workpiece when cutting several pieces of wood to the same length.

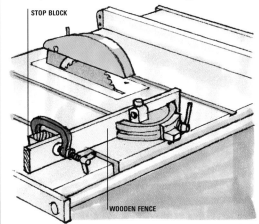

STOP BLOCK

WOODEN FENCE

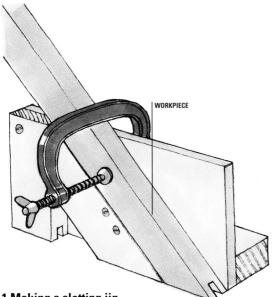

WORKPIECE

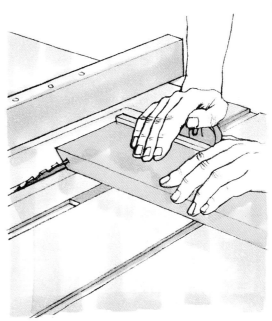

1 Making a slotting jig

To slot a flat-frame miter, make a cutting jig that will hold the work securely and keep your hands away from the saw blade. Cut an MDF backing panel about 400 x 250mm (16 x 10in). Glue and screw offcuts of the framing wood to the panel as shown, setting one to the miter angle. Ensure all screws are clear of the blade. Fix a steadying block to the opposite face of the panel, flush with the bottom edge.

Slotting a box-frame miter

Set the blade to 45 degrees and adjust it to the correct height. To position the miter accurately over the blade, butt the other end of the workpiece against a wooden block clamped to the extended miter fence.

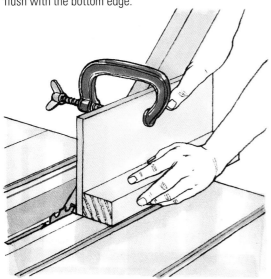

CUTTING MITERS ON A RADIAL-ARM SAW

Having sawn bevels for a box-frame miter, adjust the blade depth to saw slots for reinforcing splines across each cut face. Butt the other end of the workpiece against a stop clamped to the fence.

2 Cutting the slot

Clamp the work in the jig, with the mitered end flush with the base. Set the saw fence to center the cut on the ends. Hold the jig firmly against the fence while making the cut.

REINFORCED MITER JOINT
HAND CUT

Once you've glued up even a lightweight frame, you can drive a small brad or two into the side of the miter joints to make sure they won't come apart. Larger miter joints should be glued and allowed to set, then reinforced with veneer splines or a separate spline of solid wood or plywood.

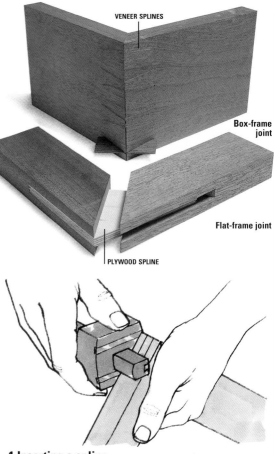

VENEER SPLINES

Box-frame joint

Flat-frame joint

PLYWOOD SPLINE

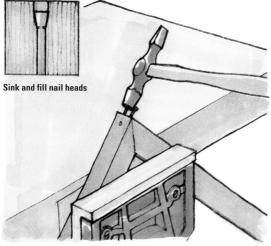

Sink and fill nail heads

Disguising a nailed joint
Sink the nail heads below the wood surface, then use matching wood filler to disguise the holes.

1 Inserting a spline
Insert a spline in a larger mitered frame. To mark a slot for the spline, set a mortise gauge to one-third the thickness of the wood, then scribe parallel lines, centered on the edges of each workpiece. Mark each end of the slot between the gauged lines, using a knife and try square.

Reinforcing with veneer
Make perpendicular or angled saw cuts across the corner of a wide miter joint; angled splines provide greater strength. Glue veneer or thin plywood splines into the saw cuts and, when set, trim them flush.

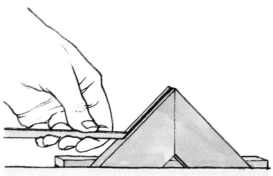

2 Fitting the spline
Set the joint vertically in a vise and saw down the waste side of the lines. Using a chisel and working from each side towards the middle, chop out the waste wood. Glue a snugly fitting spline in the slot, and trim flush when set.

BISCUIT JOINT
MACHINE CUT

A biscuit joint is a reinforced butt or miter joint. In principle, it is similar to a dowel joint, but instead of a round peg or dowel fitting in a hole, in biscuit jointing a flat oval plate (the biscuit) made of compressed beech is fitted into a matching slot. With the addition of water-based PVA glue, the biscuit expands to fill the slot, forming a very strong joint. The biscuit jointer itself is a small-scale plunge saw with a circular-saw blade, specifically developed for trimming panels or cutting grooves for drawer panels.

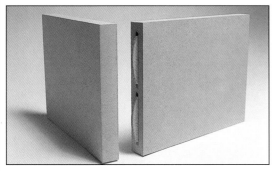

Corner butt joint

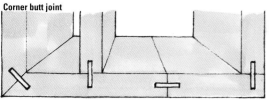

MITER JOINT   T-BUTT JOINT   EDGE-TO-EDGE JOINT   CORNER BUTT JOINT

Types of biscuit joints
You can make corner- and T-butt joints, mitered and edge-to-edge joints, in both solid wood and man-made boards. Biscuit joints are mostly used for framing or in cabinetmaking.

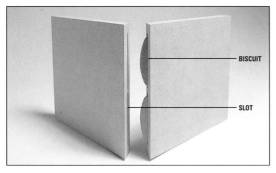

Mitered corner joint

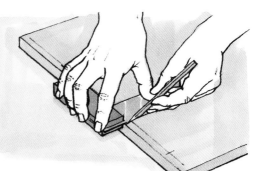

1 Marking out a corner butt joint
Draw the center line of the joint on the work, then mark along it the central point of each biscuit slot, spaced about 100mm (4in) apart. Set the cutting depth of the blade to match half the width of the biscuits being used, and adjust the tool's fence to align the blade with the marked center line.

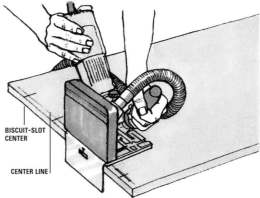

BISCUIT-SLOT CENTER

CENTER LINE

2 Cutting corner-joint slots
Before making the cut, align the cutting guide (marked on the side of the fence) with the central point of each slot. Keeping the fence pressed against the edge of the wood, switch on and plunge the blade to cut the slot.

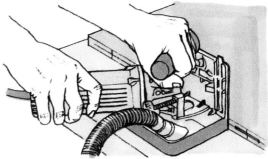

3 Cutting matching slots
To cut the other half of the joint, mark the matching biscuit-slot centers on the end of the second workpiece, and clamp it on a flat surface. Turn the guide fence over and lay the jointer on its side, then adjust the fence to center the blade on the edge of the workpiece.

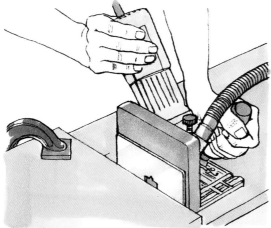

Making a T-joint

Mark the center line of the joint across one board. Use the end of the second board, clamped on its side, as a fence to align the jointer's blade with the marked line. Plunge each slot in turn. Without moving the second board, cut matching slots in its end (see page 23).

BISCUIT-JOINTER SAFETY

As well as observing the standard working methods for power tools (see page 16), note the following points with specific reference to biscuit jointers.

• Remove and throw away cracked or bent blades, and replace with sharp ones.

• The motor must be running before you plunge the blade into wood.

• Do not attempt to slow down or stop a spinning blade by applying pressure from the side.

• The blade guard must always be in place when the jointer is running.

• When cutting a groove, always feed the jointer away from you.

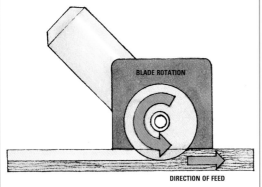

BLADE ROTATION

DIRECTION OF FEED

Using a bevel fence

Some jointers are supplied with a bevel fence for inserting biscuits in miter joints. Lay the workpiece flat on a bench, adjust the bevel fence on the jointer, and cut the slots.

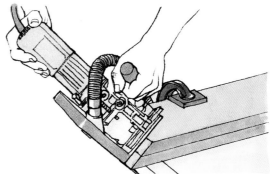

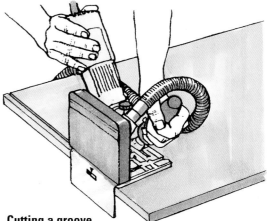

Improvising with a standard fence

Clamp the work overhanging the bench, and run the right-angle fence along the outer edge of the bevel. To help support the jointer, increase the width of the bevel by clamping one component on top of the other.

Cutting a groove

Set up the workpiece and adjust the jointer as described for making a corner-butt joint (see page 23). Rest the front end of the jointer on the panel, switch on and plunge the saw. Feed the tool across the work, then raise the blade before switching off.

CHAPTER *3* Edge joints are used to join narrow boards together to make up a large panel, such as a table top or part of a cabinet. Using modern glues, even a plain butt joint is adequate, but including a tongue and groove in the joint makes it easier to assemble accurately and adds considerably to its strength.

EDGE-TO-EDGE BUTT JOINT
HAND CUT

Timber selection is as important as good edge-to-edge joints when making a wide panel from solid wood. To ensure that the panel will remain flat, try to use quarter-sawn wood – that is, with the end-grain growth rings running perpendicular to the face side of each board. If that is not possible, arrange them so that the direction of ring growth alternates from one board to the next. Also try to ensure that the surface grain on all boards runs in the same direction, to facilitate final cleaning up of the panel with a plane. Before you get to work, number each board and mark the face side.

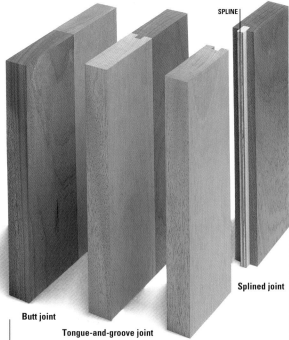

SPLINE

Butt joint

Tongue-and-groove joint

Splined joint

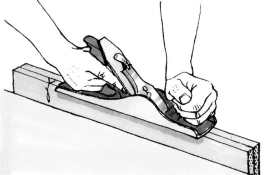

Planing edges square
With the face sides on the outside, set both boards back-to-back and level in a vise. Plane the edges straight and square, using the longest bench plane you can find, preferably a try plane.

Checking for straight edges
It is vital that the edges are straight if you intend to use a rubbed joint; check them using a metal straightedge. If the boards are to be clamped together, a very slight hollow is acceptable.

Matching edges
It is good practice to keep the edges as square as possible. However, provided boards have been planed as a pair, they will fit together and produce a flat surface, even when the edges are not exactly square.

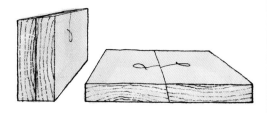

CLAMPING JOINTS
Before adding glue, set prepared boards in bar clamps to check that the joints fit snugly. Use at least three clamps, alternated as shown, to counter any tendency for the panel to bow under pressure. Use scraps of softwood to protect the edges from bruising. When you have everything to hand, remove the clamps for gluing and reassembly of the joints.

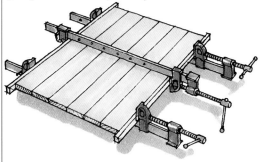

TONGUE-AND-GROOVE JOINT
HAND CUT

Use a combination plane to cut a tongue-and-groove joint by hand. This kind of plane is similar to a standard plow plane, but comes with a wider range of cutters, including one designed to shape a tongue on the edge of a workpiece. Cut the tongue first, then change the cutter and plane a matching groove.

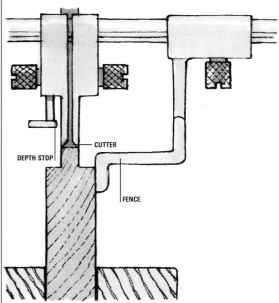

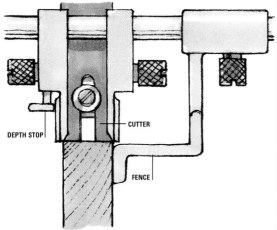

1 Adjusting the cutter
Clamp the work in a bench vise, face-side towards you. Adjust the fence until the cutter is centered on the edge of the work. Provided the matching groove is also cut from the face side, it is not essential that the tongue is precisely on-center.

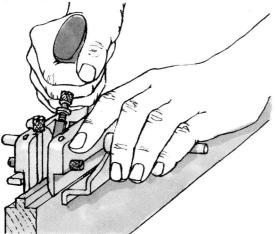

2 Cutting the tongue
Adjust the plane's depth stop to cut a tongue of the required size, then begin planing at the far end of the workpiece, gradually working backwards as the tongue is formed.

3 Cutting the groove
Select a plowing cutter that matches the width of the tongue, and fit it into the plane. Adjust the fence while sitting the cutter on top of the tongue; set the depth stop, making sure it will cut a groove slightly deeper than the tongue. Clamp the uncut board in the vise and cut the groove.

INCLUDING A SPLINE
A loose spline has three advantages over using an integral tongue; it avoids decreasing the width of the boards; it gives the joint marginally greater strength; and a simple plow plane can be used to cut the grooves. Plane a groove down the center of each board and insert a separate spline made from plywood or solid timber (ideally cross-grained). Glue one groove and tap the spline into it, then brush glue into the other groove and assemble the joint in clamps as described on page 26.

TONGUE-AND-GROOVE JOINT
MACHINE CUT

A power router is not only the perfect tool for grooving a joint to take a separate spline, it can also be adapted to machine an integral tongue on one half of a joint. For jointing larger sections of timber, consider setting up a table saw to cut tongues and grooves.

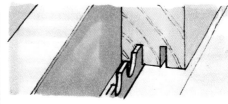

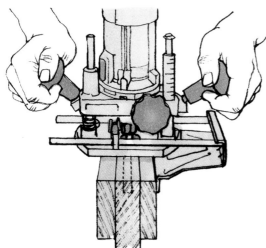

Routing the groove
A wooden strip clamped along each side of the workpiece provides a wide, flush surface to support the base of the router.

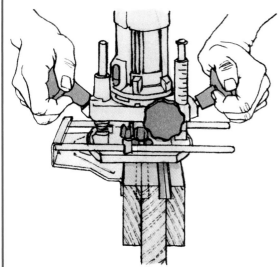

Routing an integral tongue
Clamp the matching component between two similar strips of wood, then adjust the router's fence to guide the cutter along one side of the tongue. Remove the waste from the other side.

1 Cutting a tongue with a table saw
With the wide face of the wood against the fence, saw along one side of the tongue. Turn the wood end-for-end, and saw the other side.

2 Removing waste
Adjust the fence, lay the work on its side, and cut away the waste on one side of the tongue. Turn the work over and repeat the procedure.

3 Sawing a matching groove
Adjust the fence to saw just on the inside of the groove. Turn the work end-for-end and saw down the other side of the groove before removing the waste, one saw cut at a time.

TABLE-SAW SAFETY
With some table saws, you have to remove the splitter and blade guard before you can cut a groove or rabbet; this makes operating the machine more hazardous, so work with great caution and attention. If your table saw cannot be fitted with a vertical and horizontal 'hold-down' guard, which surrounds the area of the work near the blade, make an auxiliary fence from wood, with a guard that covers the blade, to line the rip fence.

CHAPTER *4* Dowelling is just one of the methods used to reinforce butt joints. However, since a well-made dowel joint rivals the mortise and tenon in strength and versatility, it is legitimately considered to be a separate category of joint, and one which is relatively easy to make.

DOWEL JOINTS

FRAME JOINTS
HAND CUT

Frames made with dowelled butt joints are surprisingly strong. Nowadays, most factory-made furniture incorporates dowel joints, even for chair rails which must be capable of resisting prolonged and considerable strain. In most cases, two dowels per joint are sufficient. Place them a minimum of 6mm (¼in) from both edges of the rail.

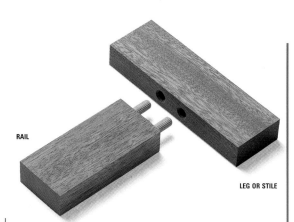

RAIL

LEG OR STILE

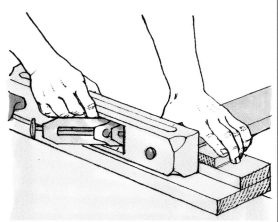

1 Cutting components to length
Saw each component to length and trim the ends of the rail square as described for making a square-ended butt joint (see page 18). Leave the stile or leg of a corner joint overlong until the joint is finished.

2 Marking the joint
Clamp the two components in a vise with their joining surfaces flush. Using a try square, draw the center of each dowel hole across both components, then scribe a line centrally on each one with a marking gauge. Bore the dowel holes where the lines cross.

3 Boring dowel holes
Place the point of a dowel bit on the marked center and bore each hole in turn. Unless you are using a dowelling jig (see opposite) or a bench stand (see page 34), it pays to have someone standing to one side who can tell you when the drill bit is vertical.

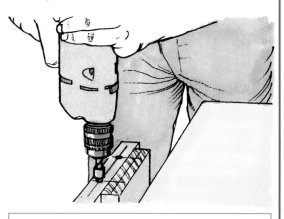

DOWELS
Ready-made dowels are manufactured from tough short-grain woods, such as ramin, birch, beech or maple. They are chamfered at each end to make them easier to insert in the holes, and are fluted length-ways to allow excess glue to escape. Choose dowels that are about half the thickness of the workpieces; the length of each dowel should be approximately five times its diameter.

If you need a few dowels only, cut them from a length of dowel rod. Steady the rod on a bench hook and cut off short sections with a fine-tooth saw. Chamfer each dowel with a file, and saw a single glue slot.

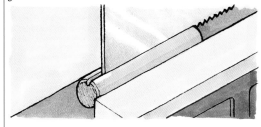

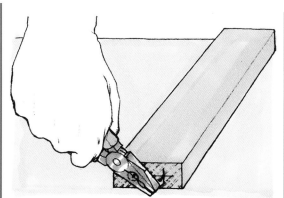

1 Using center points
For greater accuracy in marking out dowel joints, draw the center points on the end of the rail only, then drive in brads where the lines cross. Cut off the brad heads with pliers, leaving short 'spikes' projecting from the end grain.

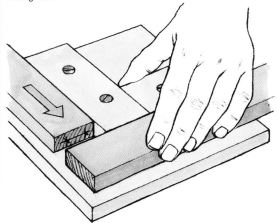

2 Marking the other component
Lay the leg or stile on its side and press the end of the rail against it, leaving two pinholes that mark the hole centers exactly. A simple right-angle jig keeps the components aligned.

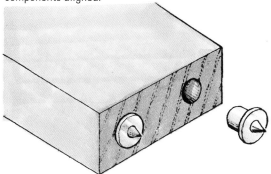

Ready-made center points
As an alternative to using brads, bore dowel holes into the end of the rail, then slip into them store-bought dowel points that will mark the side grain of the matching component.

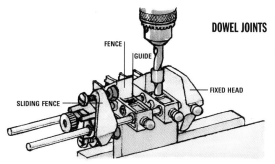

FENCE
GUIDE
FIXED HEAD
SLIDING FENCE

1 Dowelling rails with a jig
Clamp the jig on the end of the rail, ensuring that the fixed head and side fences are located against the face side and edge of the workpiece. Drill both holes.

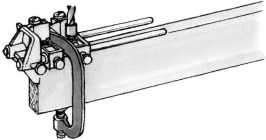

2 Dowelling the stiles
Once you have drilled all the rails, remove the sliding fence and, without altering the other settings, turn the jig over and clamp it to the stile with a C-clamp. Bore dowel holes in the side grain.

DOWELLING JIGS
It's worth acquiring a dowelling jig for a project that requires a number of identical dowel joints. The jig not only guides the bit to bore perfectly vertical holes, it also dispenses with the need to mark out each and every joint separately. With one of the better jigs, you can mark out wide boards for cabinet work as well as rails and stiles. The type of jig shown here has a fixed head or fence from which measurements are taken, and a sliding fence that clamps the jig to the work-piece. Adjustable drill-bit guides and side fences position the dowel holes.

SLIDING FENCE
DRILL-BIT GUIDE
DRILL-BIT GUIDE
FIXED HEAD

EDGE-TO-EDGE DOWEL JOINT
HAND CUT

When constructing a wide solid-wood panel, you can make a particularly strong joint between boards by inserting a dowel every 225 to 300mm (9 to 12in).

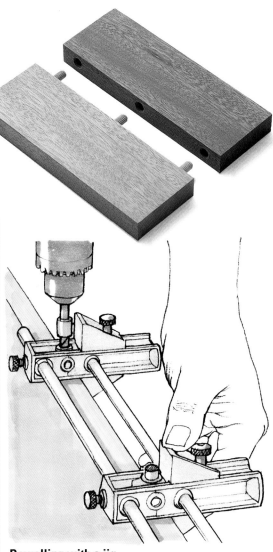

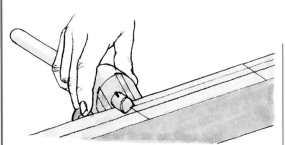

1 Marking an edge-to-edge joint
Clamp adjacent boards back-to-back in a vise and mark the dowel centers, using a try square and pencil. Scribe a line down the center of each board with a marking gauge.

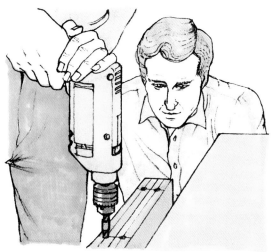

2 Boring the holes
If possible, have a helper stand at one end of the workpiece, to tell you when the drill is upright as you bore each hole where the marked lines cross.

USING A DEPTH STOP
Each hole should be slightly deeper than half the length of the dowel. To enable you to drill consistently deep holes, fit a plastic guide onto the drill bit (see right). Depth stops cost very little, but if you prefer, bind a strip of adhesive tape around the drill bit to mark the appropriate level.

Dowelling with a jig
Remove both end fences of a dowelling jig when boring holes in the edge of a wide board. Holding the side fences against the face side of the work, drill two holes. To drill subsequent holes, drop one drill-bit guide over a short dowel rod pushed into the last hole drilled.

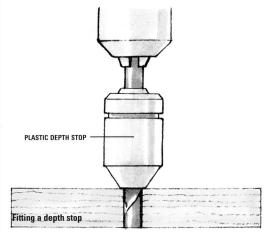

PLASTIC DEPTH STOP

Fitting a depth stop

CARCASS BUTT JOINTS
HAND CUT

When constructing a carcass with butt joints that are reinforced with multiple dowels, it pays to buy extra-long slide rods and additional drill-bit guides for a dowelling jig.

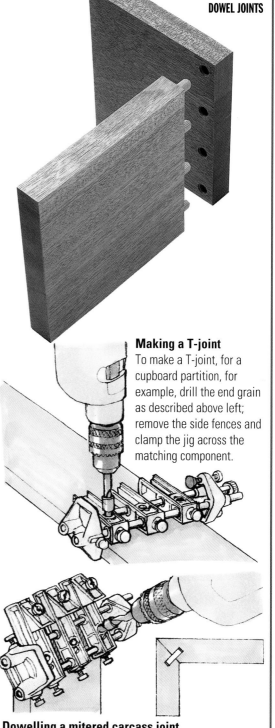

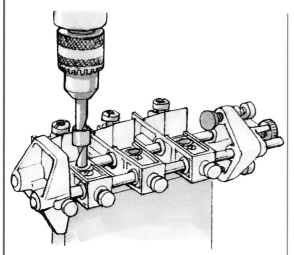

1 Dowelling a corner joint
For a right-angle butt joint, drill the end grain first. Set the jig's side fences to position the dowel holes centrally on the thickness of the workpiece, and adjust the drill-bit guides to space the dowels 50 to 75mm (2 to 3in) apart. Make sure the fixed head is clamped against the face edge.

Making a T-joint
To make a T-joint, for a cupboard partition, for example, drill the end grain as described above left; remove the side fences and clamp the jig across the matching component.

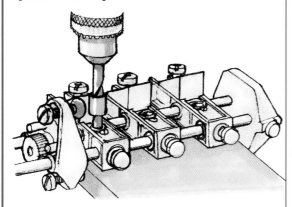

2 Drilling matching holes
Without changing any settings, invert the jig and clamp it to the inside of the other component, with the side fences butted against the end grain and the fixed head against the face edge. Attach a depth stop (see opposite) to the bit to ensure you don't drill right through the wood.

Dowelling a mitered carcass joint
To make a dowel-reinforced miter joint, assemble a jig similar to that used for a right-angle butt joint (see left), and clamp it to the bevelled end of the workpiece. Adjust the drill-bit guides to position the dowels towards the lower edge of the bevel. Having drilled the dowel holes, transfer the jig to the other mitered board and drill matching holes.

33

DOWEL JOINTS
MACHINE CUT

A drill press, or even a power drill mounted in a sturdy drill stand, solves the problem of drilling dowel holes vertically. All you have to do is ensure that the work is positioned accurately before you pull down on the lever.

For an edge-to-edge joint, for example, bolt a simple fence to the base so that you can slide the work along it until each marked hole center is directly below the tip of the dowel bit. The depth gauge on the stand will prevent the drill boring too deeply into the work. Chamfering the holes makes final assembly easier.

Make a special jig for the drill stand when you want to make several dowelled frame joints.

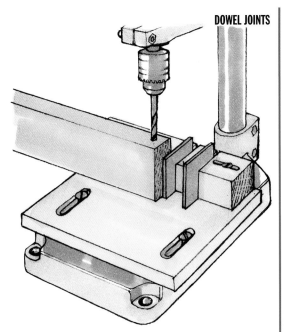

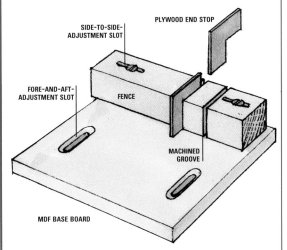

SIDE-TO-SIDE-
ADJUSTMENT SLOT

PLYWOOD END STOP

FORE-AND-AFT-
ADJUSTMENT SLOT

FENCE

MACHINED
GROOVE

MDF BASE BOARD

Making a corner-joint jig
To join a rail and stile at right angles, make a simple jig comprising a 12mm (½in) MDF baseboard and a hard-wood fence with adjustable end stops.

1 Cut slots in the baseboard to provide fore-and-aft adjustment when bolted to the drill-stand base.

2 Machine 10mm (⅜in) deep grooves in the top and sides of the fence to take 3mm (⅛in) thick plywood end stops. Set them apart to provide the required spacing between dowel holes. Make L-shape plywood stops that fit snugly in the grooves.

3 Machine bolt slots in the fence for side-to-side adjustment once the fence is bolted flush with the back edge of the baseboard.

Boring dowel holes in a stile
Adjust the jig to position the center line of the stile directly below the drill bit. With the end of the workpiece butted against the first plywood stop, bore the hole for the dowel. Remove the stop and slide the work up to the second end stop, then bore another dowel hole.

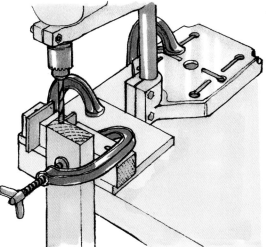

Boring holes in the end of a rail
To allow you to set the rail vertically, swing the drill stand to overhang the bench, and clamp it down. Clamp the workpiece to the jig, then the jig to the bench, in order to position the end grain below the dowel bit. Drill the first hole, remove the stop, then reposition the work against the second stop and drill another hole.

CHAPTER 5 The bridle joint is similar in appearance to a mortise-and-tenon joint, though in most circumstances it would not be as strong. However, a bridle joint is relatively quick and easy to make, since most of the waste wood is removed with a saw. The 'tenon' of a bridle joint, which is used exclusively for frame construction, usually constitutes one-third the thickness of the wood being joined.

BRIDLE JOINTS

CORNER BRIDLE JOINT
HAND CUT

A corner bridle joint is adequate for relatively lightweight frames, provided they are not subjected to sideways pressure, which tends to force bridle joints out of square. The strength of the bridle is improved considerably if you insert two dowels through the side of the joint after the glue has set.

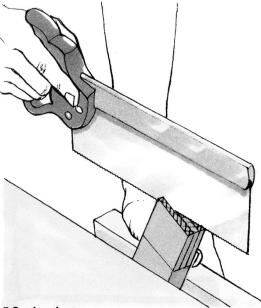

TENON MEMBER

MORTISE MEMBER

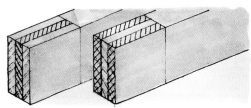

1 Marking out the shoulders
Taking each tenon member in turn, mark square shoulders all round, allowing for a tenon that is slightly overlong so that it can be planed flush after the joint is complete. Use a marking knife, but apply light pressure across both edges. Mark out the mortise member similarly, but this time use a pencil.

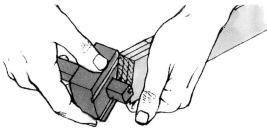

2 Scribing the tenon
Set the points of a mortise gauge to one-third the thickness of the wood, and adjust the tool's stock (fence) to center the points on the edge of the work. Scribe the width of the tenon on both edges and across the end.

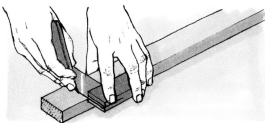

3 Marking out the open mortise
Use the same gauge to mark the sides of the open mortise, then take a marking knife and score the short shoulders at the base of the mortise, between the gauged lines. Mark the waste wood with a pencil on both components so that you don't get confused when cutting the joint.

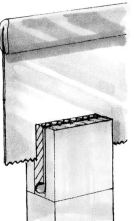

4 Cutting the open mortise
Select a drill bit that approximates the width of the mortise, and bore a hole into the waste wood just above the shoulder line on opposite sides of the joint. Set the wood in a vise and saw on the waste side of both gauged lines, down to the hole at the base of the mortise. Chisel the shoulder square.

5 Cutting the tenon
With the work clamped in a vise, saw both sides of the tenon down to the shoulder (see mortise and tenon, page 65). Lay the workpiece on its side on a bench hook and saw each shoulder line to remove the waste wood.

CORNER BRIDLE JOINT
MACHINE CUT

A table saw is perhaps the best machine for cutting bridle joints. It is good practice to fit the blade guard whenever possible; however, if a particular operation requires you to remove it, always use a jig that will permit you to perform the task safely, keeping your hands away from the blade.

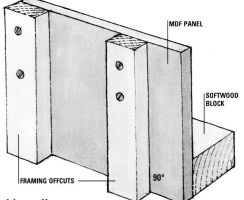

MDF PANEL

SOFTWOOD BLOCK

FRAMING OFFCUTS   90°

Making a jig
Most relatively sophisticated table saws have tenon-cutting jigs for securing workpieces and guiding them past the blade. In the absence of such equipment, make a jig that will hold the wood upright while it is run along the rip fence.

1 Cutting the tenon
With the saw blade set to the same height, adjust the fence to place the blade just to the waste side of the tenon. Make the first cut, reverse the work in the jig, and make a second pass over the blade.

Cutting an open mortise
Having cut the component to length, clamp it vertically in the jig. Adjust the fence to saw just on the inside of the mortise, and raise the blade to make the required depth of cut. Make the first cut, reverse the work in the jig, and pass it across the blade again, to saw down the other side of the mortise. If necessary, reset the saw fence to remove any remaining waste.

2 Sawing the shoulders
Clamp a block of wood to the saw fence and, with the end of the workpiece butted against the block, adjust the fence to place the blade just to the waste side of the shoulder. Adjust the blade height to just remove the waste. Using the miter fence, pass the work over the blade – the spacer block prevents the waste jamming against the fence. Turn the work over and make a second pass.

MITERED BRIDLE JOINT
HAND CUT

The mitered bridle is cut in a similar way to the conventional corner joint, but is a more attractive alternative for framing, because end grain appears on one edge only.

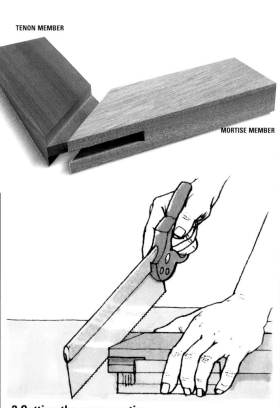

TENON MEMBER

MORTISE MEMBER

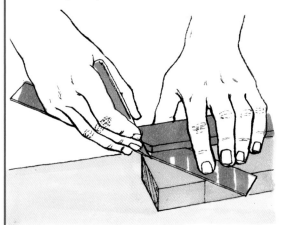

1 Marking the joint
Cut the components exactly to length. Mark the width of the parts on each end and square the shoulders all round, using a try square and pencil. Mark the sloping face of the miter on both sides of each component with a knife and miter square.

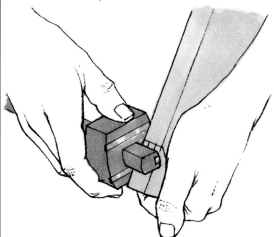

2 Gauging the tenon and open mortise
Set the pins of a mortise gauge to one-third the thickness of the wood, and adjust the stock to centralize the pair of pins on the edge of the work. Scribe the width of the tenon on the inside edge and across the end grain of the appropriate member. On the mortise member, scribe similar lines across the end and on both edges.

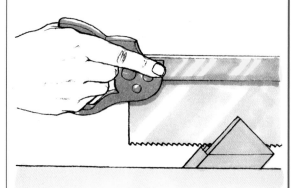

3 Cutting the open mortise
Cut out the waste from the mortise as described for a conventional corner bridle joint (see page 36), then hold the work on a bench hook and saw down the marked line to miter both cheeks of the joint. If the miters are not perfect, shave them with a block plane.

4 Cutting the tenon
Clamp the tenon member at an angle in a vise and saw down to the mitered shoulder on both sides of the tenon; keep the saw blade just to the waste side of the line. Holding the work on a bench hook, saw along both mitered shoulders to remove the waste. If necessary, trim the mitered surfaces with a shoulder plane.

CANVAS-STRETCHER JOINT
HAND CUT

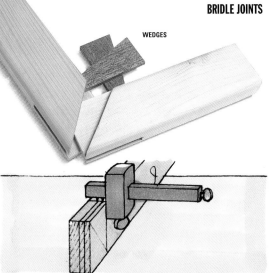

WEDGES

Traditionally, most paintings are made on canvas stretched over a wooden frame. Ready-made frames are expensive, and it is worth making your own, using a variation of the mitered bridle joint. The frame is assembled without glue so that, if the canvas becomes slack due to changes in humidity, tension can be applied by driving wedges inside each corner of the frame to expand the joints.
In the following instructions, the face side of each piece of wood, or 'stretcher', refers to the surface that faces the canvas. Descriptions of right- and left-hand ends of a stretcher mean when they are seen from face side.

1 Marking the square shoulders
Cut four stretchers to length. Draw square shoulders all round, one stretcher-width from each end.

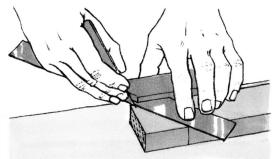

2 Marking the mitered shoulders
Using a miter square and knife, score a diagonal from the outer corners on both sides of the stretcher

3 Gauging the open mortise and tenon
Set the pins of a mortise gauge to one-quarter of the thickness of the wood. Adjust the stock to place the outermost, fixed pin on the center line. Working from the face side, scribe two parallel lines on both edges and across the end grain at the left-hand end of each

stretcher. On the inside edge only, extend the lines past the shoulder by 9mm (⅜in), to accommodate wedges at a later stage.
   At the right-hand end of each stretcher, scribe lines across the end grain and along the inside edge only, stopping at the shoulder.

4 Resetting the mortise gauge
Reset the gauge to place the innermost pin on the center line. Mark both ends of each stretcher in a similar way, but this time scribe both edges and end grain at the right-hand end (allowing for wedges), and only the end grain and inside edge at the left-hand end.

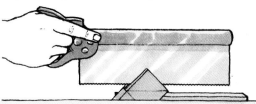

5 Cutting the joint
Mark the waste clearly with pencil, to avoid confusion. Saw out the waste, following the gauged lines and mitered-shoulder lines. Plane a small radius along the edges of the stretchers, and plane the face sides to a shallow bevel, sloping towards the inner edges. This prevents the wood marking the canvas.
   Once the canvas is stretched over the frame, apply tension by driving two shallow wedges per joint into the slots left on the inside of each corner.

T-BRIDLE JOINT
HAND CUT

The T-bridle serves as an intermediate support for a frame and, with modifications, is sometimes used to joint a table leg to the underframe when a long rail requires support. Unlike the corner bridle, which is relatively weak under sideways pressure, the T-bridle is similar in strength to the mortise-and-tenon joint.

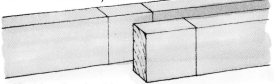

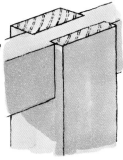

MORTISE MEMBER

TENON MEMBER

1 Marking the shoulders
Mark the width of the mortise member on the tenon member, using a marking knife to score square shoulders all round. Apply light pressure only across the edges. Allowing for slightly overlong cheeks on the mortise member, mark square shoulders all round with a pencil and try square.

2 Gauging the joint
Set the pins of a mortise gauge to one-third the thickness of the wood, and adjust the stock to center the pair of pins on the edge of the workpiece. Scribe parallel lines between the marked shoulders on the tenon member, then mark similar lines on the end and both edges of the mortise member.

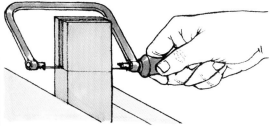

3 Cutting the open mortise
Cut the mortise as described for a corner bridle joint (see page 36). Alternatively, saw down both sides of the open mortise with a tenon saw, then use a coping saw to remove the waste, cutting as close to the shoulder as possible. If necessary, trim the shoulder square with a sharp chisel.

4 Cutting the tenon member
On both sides of the tenon member, saw the shoulders down to the gauged lines, then make three or four similar saw cuts in between. With the work held firmly, chop out the waste with a mallet and chisel, working from each edge towards the middle. Having assembled the joint, allow the glue to set, then plane the ends of the mortise cheeks flush with the tenon member.

TABLE-LEG VERSION
When joining a square leg to a table underframe, make the 'tenon' about two-thirds the thickness of the rail. Offset the open mortise so that a slightly overhanging table top can conceal the leg's end grain.

40

CHAPTER **6** A rabbet joint is a simple corner joint used to construct box frames and small cabinets. The basic joint requires the ability to plane the ends of workpieces perfectly square and cut a rabbet across the grain. It is only moderately strong, and requires reinforcing with brads or modifying to include a tongue and groove to improve its rigidity.

RABBET JOINTS

RABBET JOINT
HAND CUT

A basic rabbet joint is only marginally stronger than a straightforward butt joint, but it is an improvement in appearance, since most of the end grain is concealed. As a result, it is sometimes used as a relatively simple way of connecting a drawer front to drawer sides.

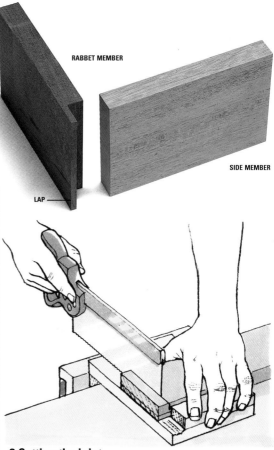

RABBET MEMBER

SIDE MEMBER

LAP

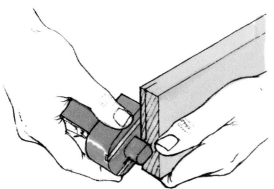

1 Marking out the rabbet
Cut and plane both members square. Adjust a marking gauge to about one-quarter of the thickness of the rabbet member, and scribe a line across the end grain, working from the face side. Continue the line on both edges, down to the level of the shoulder.

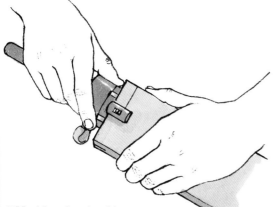

2 Marking the shoulder
Set a cutting gauge to match the thickness of the side member, and scribe a shoulder line parallel to the end grain on the back of the rabbet member. Continue the shoulder line across both edges to meet the lines already scribed.

3 Cutting the joint
Clamp the rabbet member upright in a vise. Following the line scribed across the end grain, saw down to the shoulder line. Lay the work face-down on a bench hook and cut down the shoulder line with a tenon saw to remove the waste. Make a neat joint by cleaning up the rabbet with a shoulder plane.

4 Assembling the joint
Glue and clamp the joint, then drive brads or small finish nails through the side member. Sink the brads with a nail set and fill the holes.

RABBET JOINT
MACHINE CUT

Because it is made with simple saw cuts, the rabbet joint is particularly easy to produce with a table saw or radial-arm saw.

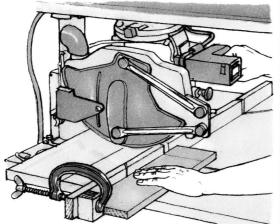

Cutting to length on a radial-arm saw
Holding each component against the fence, pull the saw towards you to cut one end square. Turn the work over and sever the other end. When sawing several identical pieces, clamp an end stop to the fence to save you having to measure each workpiece.

Cutting to length on a table saw
Cut square both ends of each workpiece. When cutting identical pieces to length, attach an extension to the table saw's miter fence and clamp an end stop to it (see page 20).

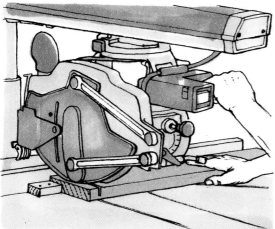

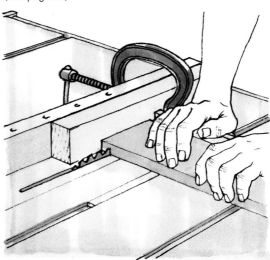

Sawing the rabbet
Adjust the blade to cut three-quarters through the workpiece. Mark the shoulder on the back of the rabbet member, then align it with the blade to cut just to the waste side of the line. Having cut the shoulder, slide the work sideways one blade-width at a time, gradually removing the waste. To cut identical shoulders, align the squared end of the wood with a pencil line drawn on the fence, or butt the end against a block nailed temporarily to the saw's worktable.

Cutting the rabbet
Adjust the blade height to saw three-quarters through the workpiece. Butt the end of the work against a spacer block clamped to the saw's rip fence, then adjust the fence to saw just to the waste side of the shoulder line. Make a short trial cut to check the accuracy of your settings, then pass the work over the blade. Slide the work sideways away from the rip fence to remove the waste in stages (see left).

MITERED RABBET JOINT
HAND CUT

A mitered rabbet joint is somewhat neater than the basic version, but is more difficult to cut.

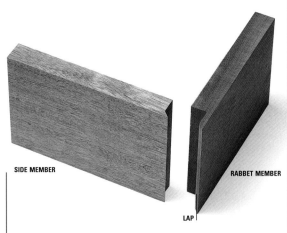

SIDE MEMBER

RABBET MEMBER

LAP

1 Marking and cutting the miter
Mark out and cut the rabbet as described for the basic joint (see page 42), then use a miter square and marking knife to score a 45-degree miter on the end of the projecting lap. Score a line across the inside of the lap to mark the base of the miter, and carefully plane off the waste down to this line.

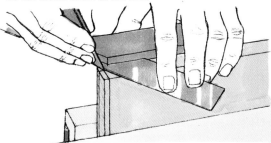

2 Marking the side member
Set a cutting gauge to the thickness of the lap, and use it to scribe a shoulder line across the inside and both edges of the side member. Then, with the stock of the same gauge pressed against the face side, scribe a line across the end grain and down each edge to meet the shoulder line. Mark the slope of the miter from the outer corner down to the shoulder line.

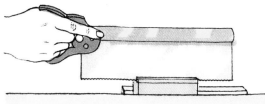

3 Sawing the waste
Set the workpiece upright in a vise and, following the line scribed across the end grain, saw down to meet the shoulder line. Then, holding the side member face-down on a bench hook, saw down the shoulder line to remove the waste.

4 Planing the miter
Use a shoulder plane to trim the miter, clamping a backing board bevelled to 45 degrees behind the work, to help guide the sole of the plane.

DOWELLED MITER JOINT
Use stopped dowels if you want to strengthen the joint without any obvious form of reinforcement.

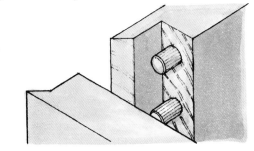

HALF-BLIND TONGUE-AND-RABBET JOINT
MACHINE CUT

The half-blind tongue-and-rabbet joint can be cut on a table saw (see page 46), or with a power router as described here. It is sometimes used by woodworkers as a substitute for the half-blind dovetail in drawer construction, but it is not nearly as strong. When making the joint, prepare and sand the work beforehand, since any change in size afterwards will result in a loose joint.

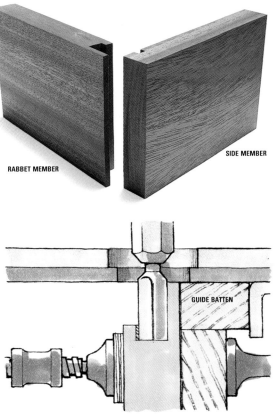

RABBET MEMBER

SIDE MEMBER

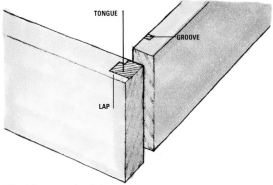

TONGUE

GROOVE

LAP

Marking out the joint
In order to visualize the joint and help you set up the router, mark out the joint first on one pair of components. Other identical joints will not require marking. The lap on the rabbet member should be about 4 to 6mm (³⁄₁₆ to ¼in) thick. Choose a router cutter of a similar diameter to machine the groove in the side member, and plan to cut it to a similar depth.

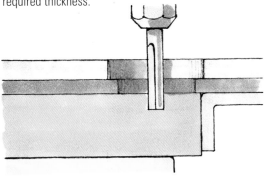

GUIDE BATTEN

2 Machining the rabbet member – second cut
Clamp the work upright in a vise. To help steady the router, clamp a guide batten to the face side, flush with the end grain. Adjust the router fence to trim the lap to the required thickness, and set the depth of cut to remove the remaining waste. Reset the fence to make another pass with the cutter, leaving the tongue at the required thickness.

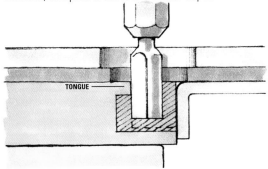

TONGUE

1 Machining the rabbet member – first cut
Clamp the workpiece face-down on the bench. Adjust the router fence until the cutter will remove the waste up to the end of the tongue. Remove the waste in stages, stopping just short of the lap. You can machine several identical components at once if you clamp them side-by-side, flat on the bench.

3 Cutting the groove
Set the depth of cut to match the length of the tongue, and adjust the fence to place the groove the required distance from the end of the workpiece. Make the cut with a single pass. Once again, you can save time by machining several workpieces at once.

LOCK MITER JOINT
MACHINE CUT

The lock miter is similar to the half-blind tongue-and-rabbet joint, but is made with a small miter that conceals the end grain, or the core of suitable man-made boards, at the corner. The joint can be cut entirely on a table saw – using a dado head enables you to cut the joint quickly, but you can remove the waste in stages using a conventional saw blade.

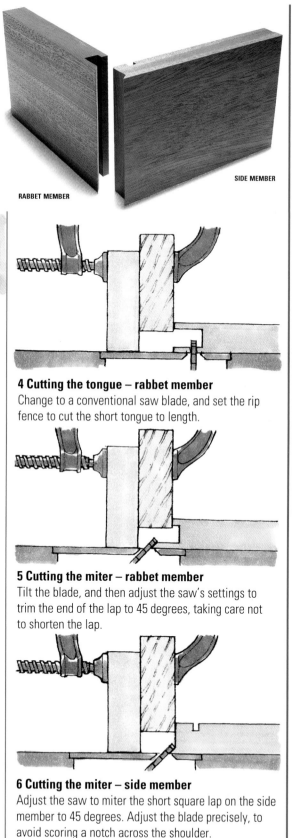

RABBET MEMBER

SIDE MEMBER

THICKNESS OF WOOD

1 Cutting the groove – side member
Cut the groove across the side member with a single pass across the circular saw blade.

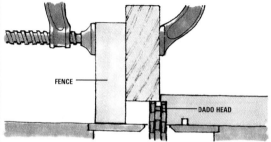

FENCE

DADO HEAD

2 Cutting the rabbet – side member
Set up the saw with a dado head and adjust the height to remove enough waste to leave a short square lap that will form the miter at a later stage. Clamp a wooden spacer to the rip fence, just above the dado head, against which you can butt the end of the work.

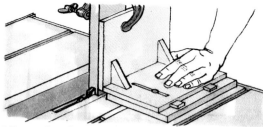

3 Removing the waste – rabbet member
Adjust the saw and use a dado head that will leave a lap that is about one-quarter of the wood's thickness, and a tongue on the inside that will fit the groove cut in the side member. Set the height of the dado head to match the thickness of the side member. Then clamp the rabbet member upright in a tenon-cutting jig (see page 80), and remove the waste with one pass across the saw blade.

4 Cutting the tongue – rabbet member
Change to a conventional saw blade, and set the rip fence to cut the short tongue to length.

5 Cutting the miter – rabbet member
Tilt the blade, and then adjust the saw's settings to trim the end of the lap to 45 degrees, taking care not to shorten the lap.

6 Cutting the miter – side member
Adjust the saw to miter the short square lap on the side member to 45 degrees. Adjust the blade precisely, to avoid scoring a notch across the shoulder.

CHAPTER 7 A dado is a groove cut across the grain. When used as a joint, it houses the end of a board, most frequently a fixed shelf or dividing panel. The dado itself is either stopped short of the front edge of the work or, for less-important work, the joint may emerge as a through dado. The shelf or panel is usually glued into a simple straight-sided dado. However, for a more positive joint, a dovetail can be included.

THROUGH DADO JOINT
HAND CUT

This simple through joint shows on the front edges of side panels. It is suitable for rough shelving, or for cupboards with lay-on doors that cover the front edges. If you plan to lip the boards, it is best to apply the lippings first, so it is easier to plane them flush.

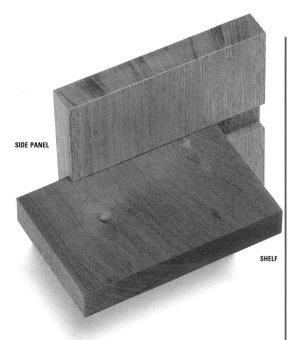

SIDE PANEL

SHELF

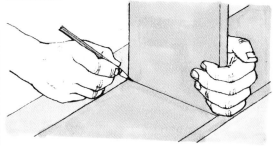

1 Marking the face of the side panel
Measure the width of the dado from the shelf, then score the two lines across the workpiece, using a try square and marking knife.

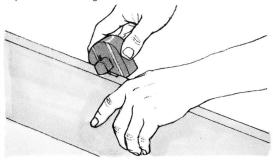

2 Marking the edges
Square the same lines onto the edges of the panel, then scribe a line between them, using a marking gauge set to about 6mm (¼in).

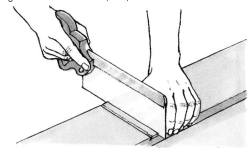

3 Sawing the dado shoulders
To make it easier to locate a saw across a wide panel, take a chisel and pare a shallow V-shape groove up to the marked line on both sides of the dado, then use a tenon saw to cut each shoulder down to the lines scribed on each edge.

4 Removing the waste
Pare out the waste from a narrow panel with a chisel, working from each side towards the middle.

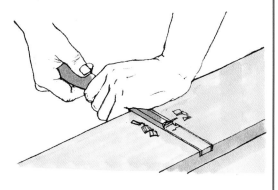

USING A ROUTER PLANE
Having chiselled out most of the waste, pare the bottom of a dado level, using a special router plane fitted with a narrow, adjustable L-shape blade. When a panel is too wide to use a chisel conveniently, remove all the waste in stages by making several passes with the router plane, lowering the cutter each time the dado is level.

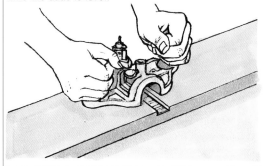

STRAIGHT SLIDING DOVETAIL
HAND CUT

When cutting this joint by hand, incorporate a single dovetail along one side of the dado. Double-sided dovetails are best cut with a router (see page 51). Since the shelf member must be slid into place from one end of the dado, the joint needs to be cut accurately.

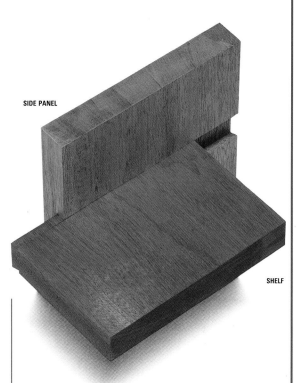

SIDE PANEL

SHELF

1 Marking the shoulder
Set a cutting gauge to about one-third the thickness of the wood and score a shoulder line on the underside of the shelf. Using a try square and pencil, continue the line across both edges.

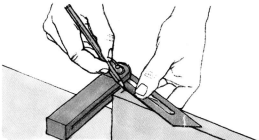

2 Marking the dovetail angle
Set a sliding bevel to a dovetail angle (see page 82), and mark the slope of the joint, running from the bottom corner to the marks drawn on both edges.

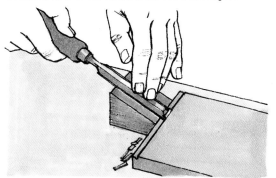

3 Paring the slope
Saw along the shoulder line, down to the base of the slope, then pare out the waste with a chisel. To help keep the angle constant, use a shaped block of wood to guide the blade.

4 Cutting the dado
Mark out the dado as described opposite, and use the sliding bevel to mark the dovetail on both edges of the panel. Saw both shoulders, using a bevelled block of wood to guide the saw blade when cutting the dovetail. Remove the waste with a router plane, or use a bevel-edge chisel to clear the undercut.

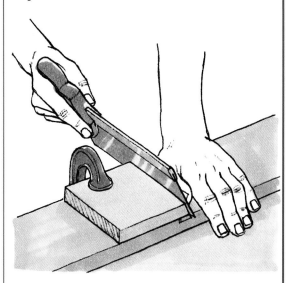

STOPPED DADO JOINT
HAND CUT

For decorative effect, the dado is often stopped short of the front edge of the side panel by about 9 to 12mm ($\frac{3}{8}$ to $\frac{1}{2}$in). Occasionally, the shelf is also cut short, fitting the dado exactly – useful when making a cupboard with inset doors. Generally, however, the front edge of the shelf is notched so that its front edge finishes flush with the side panel. The instructions below explain how to cut the joint with handtools, but a power router is perhaps the ideal tool for cutting a stopped dado (see opposite).

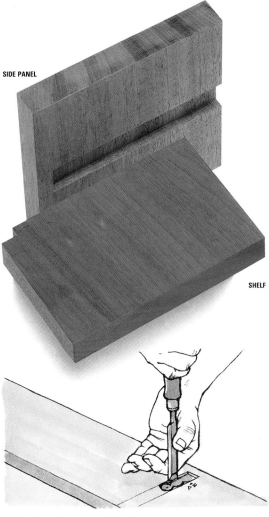

SIDE PANEL

SHELF

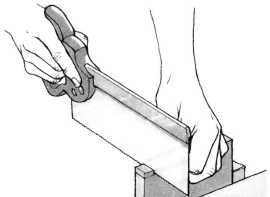

1 Notching the shelf
Set a marking gauge to the planned depth of the dado, and use it to mark the notch on the front corner of the shelf. Cut the notch with a tenon saw.

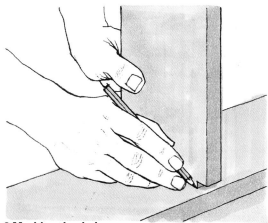

2 Marking the dado
Use the notched shelf to mark the dimensions of the dado, then score the lines across the side panel with a try square and marking knife. Scribe the stopped end of the dado with a marking gauge.

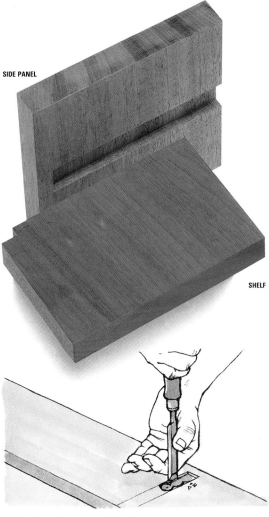

3 Cutting the stopped end
To provide clearance for sawing the dado, first drill out the waste at the stopped end and trim the shoulders square with a chisel.

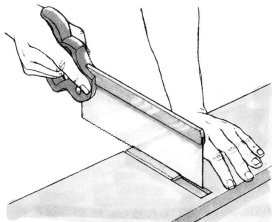

4 Sawing the dado
Saw along the scored shoulders down to the base of the dado, then pare out the waste from the back edge with a chisel, or use a router plane.

STOPPED STRAIGHT SLIDING DOVETAIL JOINT
MACHINE CUT

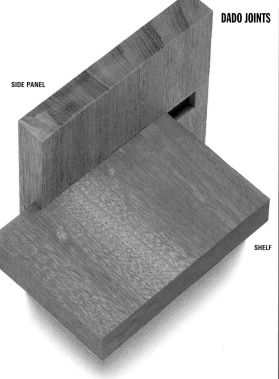

SIDE PANEL

SHELF

You can cut any form of dado joint with a power router, and there is no better tool for machining the fully dovetailed version. The cutter removes the waste and shapes the sides of the dado in one operation. Use a wooden straightedge clamped to the work as a guide for the router or, to make it easier to repeat similar dados, make a T-square from wood. One advantage of using a dovetailed dado is that the shelf can be sanded after the joint has been cut, without it resulting in a loose fit.

MAKING A T-SQUARE

Prepare 150 x 12mm (6 x ½in) straight-grained hardwood, and cut from it a 600mm (2ft) T-square blade. Cut a 400mm (1ft 4in) stock from 75 x 12mm (3 x ½in) wood. Screw and glue the blade to the stock at 90 degrees. Mark both ends of the stock with a line that is the same distance from the edge of the T-square blade as the center of the router cutter is from the edge of the tool's base. Use these lines to position the cutter on the center line of the dado.

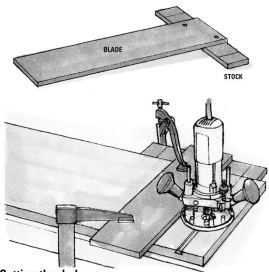

BLADE

STOCK

Cutting the dado
Align the mark on the T-square stock with the center line of the dado pencilled across the workpiece. Clamp the T-square onto the work. Adjust the router cutter to the required depth (about one-third the thickness of the wood), then machine the dado, stopping about 12mm (½in) from the front edge of the panel. Square the end of the dado with a chisel.

Machining the shelf
Set the work upright in a vise and clamp an L-shape guide batten on each side, flush with the end grain. Adjust the side fence to machine a dovetail along one side of the work, then reset the fence to dovetail the other side.

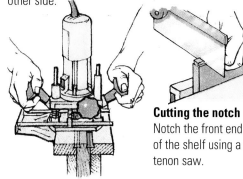

Cutting the notch
Notch the front end of the shelf using a tenon saw.

USING A ROUTER TABLE
As an alternative method of cutting the dovetail, invert the router in a worktable, and set the table's fence to guide the workpiece past the cutter. Having made one pass, reverse the work and dovetail the other face.

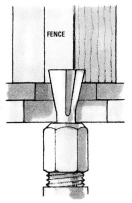

FENCE

SLIDING DOVETAIL JOINT
HAND CUT

The sliding dovetail is a variant of the stopped dado, having a dovetail slope along one side, but also tapering towards the stopped end. It is particularly useful for deep cabinets, because it remains slack while you assemble the joint, finally pulling itself tight at the last moment. However, it requires very precise making to achieve the desired result.

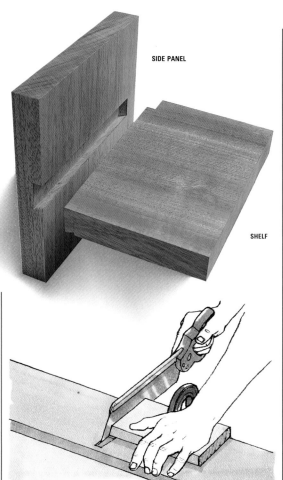

SIDE PANEL

SHELF

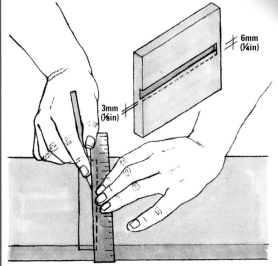

6mm (¼in)

3mm (⅛in)

1 Marking the dado
Pencil a straight-sided, stopped dado on the side panel, then rule a line representing the tapered shoulder of the housing. Allow for the dovetail by starting the line 3mm (⅛in) above the lower shoulder at the back end of the dado, and then tapering to 6mm (¼in) above the line at the stopped end.

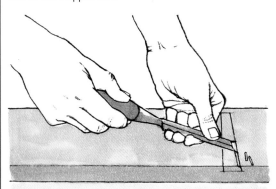

2 Chiselling grooves along the shoulders
Deeply score both the square and tapering shoulders with a marking knife, then chisel out the waste up to the scored lines, forming shallow V-shape grooves.

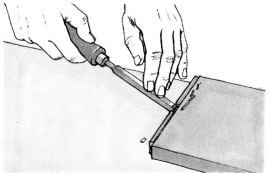

3 Sawing the shoulders
Chop out the waste from the stopped dado end to provide saw-blade clearance, then cut both shoulders with a saw. Undercut the tapering shoulder to an angle of 80 degrees, using a shaped block to guide the blade. Pare out the waste and level the dado with a router plane.

4 Dovetailing the shelf end
Mark the shoulder line on the underside of the shelf, using a cutting gauge, and mark the taper on the end grain, taking the dimensions from the dado. Cut out the notch at the stopped end, and saw along the shoulder line. Pare out the waste with a chisel, following the dovetail angle. Try assembling the joint, and relieve any tight spots until it fits snugly.

TONGUE-AND-RABBET JOINT
HAND CUT

The tongue-and-rabbet joint is a variation on the basic rabbet joint, adapted for making box-frame or cabinet corners. The dado should be no deeper than about one-quarter the thickness of the wood, and about the same in width.

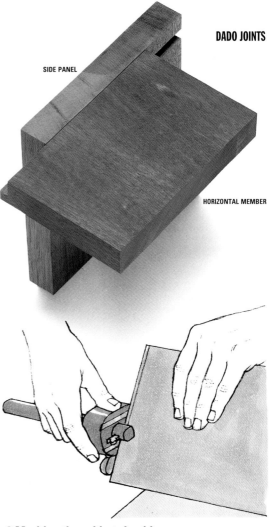

SIDE PANEL

HORIZONTAL MEMBER

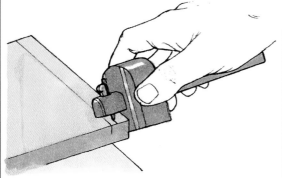

1 Marking the dado
Cut and plane square the ends of both components. Set a cutting gauge to the thickness of the horizontal member, and lightly scribe the bottom edge of the dado across the side panel and down both edges. Reset the gauge and scribe the top edge of the dado in the same way.

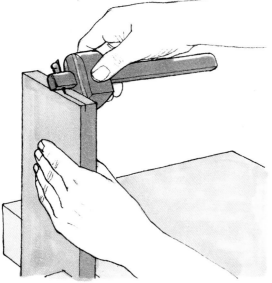

2 Marking the tongue
Using the gauge with the same setting, mark the tongue on the end and down both edges of the horizontal member, working from the face side.

3 Marking the rabbet shoulder
Re-set the gauge to about one-third the thickness of the side panel, and mark the rabbet shoulder line across the face side and down both edges of the horizontal member. Form the rabbet by removing the waste with a saw and cleaning up with a shoulder plane.

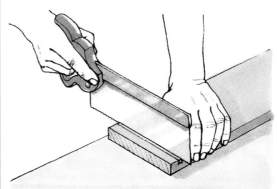

4 Cutting the dado
Mark the depth of the dado on the edges of the side panel and remove the waste with a saw and chisel, as described for cutting a through dado joint (see page 48).

TONGUE-AND-RABBET JOINT
MACHINE CUT

The simplicity of the tongue-and-rabbet joint lends itself to cutting by machine. You could use a router for cutting the dado, or use a table saw, as shown here, for cutting the entire joint. You may need a dado head (see page 122) to make a wide cut, or you can fit an adjustable dado blade which cants the saw blade to a slight angle, making a wider-than-normal kerf as the blade rotates.

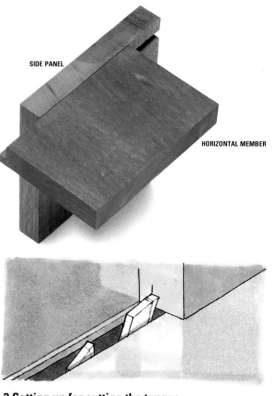

SIDE PANEL

HORIZONTAL MEMBER

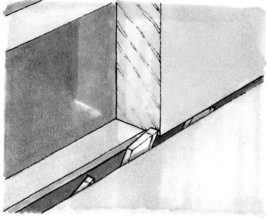

1 Setting up for cutting the dado
Using the horizontal member as a guide, set the rip fence to place the saw blade flush with the outside face of the wood. If you are using an adjustable dado blade, check that the blade is canted to its full extent.

2 Cutting the dado
Raise the blade to one-quarter of the side-panel thickness. Lay the side panel flat on the saw table, its end butted against the rip fence, and pass the work over the blade. Adjust the rip fence sideways to make a second cut for a wider dado. Use the saw's miter fence to steady a narrow workpiece.

3 Setting up for cutting the tongue
Mark the width of the tongue on the horizontal member, using the dado as a template. Reset the rip fence to cut just to the waste side of the mark.

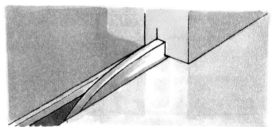

4 Cutting the tongue
Holding the work on end, run the horizontal panel against the fence to cut a kerf alongside the tongue. Use a jig (see page 37) to support a narrow workpiece.

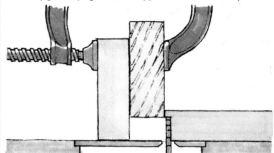

5 Cutting the rabbet shoulder
Clamp a wooden spacer to the rip fence; the end of the tongue will run against this. Raise the saw blade and adjust the fence to cut the rabbet, leaving a tongue that will fit the dado precisely.

CHAPTER 8 Half-lap joints are employed exclusively for framing, using wood of equal thickness for both components of a joint. They are very easy to cut, even with handtools, and the basic joint can be adapted to make right-angle corners, T-joints and cross frames.

HALF-LAP JOINTS

CROSS LAP JOINT
HAND CUT

With a cross lap joint, both halves of the joint are identical. Although the joint is equally strong whichever way the components run, convention dictates that the vertical member or divider appears to run through, although, in reality, half the thickness is removed from each piece of wood.

RAIL

DIVIDER

1 Marking the shoulders
Lay both components side-by-side and score the shoulder lines across them, using a try square and marking knife. Continue both sets of marked lines half-way down each edge.

2 Marking the depth of the joint
Set a marking gauge to exactly half the thickness of the wood, and scribe a line between the shoulders marked on the edges of both components.

3 Cutting the joint
Saw halfway through both pieces of wood on the waste side of each shoulder line. Divide the waste wood between the shoulders with one or two additional saw cuts.

4 Chopping out the waste
Clamp the work in a vise and chisel out the waste, working from each side towards the middle of each component. Pare the bottom of each resulting recess flat with a chisel.

USING A TABLE SAW
Adjust the saw blade to cut halfway through the workpiece. Saw one shoulder, then slide the wood sideways and saw the second one. To cut identical shoulders on several pieces of wood, set up the saw so that you can butt each workpiece against the rip fence at one end and against a block of wood clamped to the miter fence at the other. Remove the waste by making several passes across the blade.

GLAZING-BAR LAP JOINT
HAND CUT

Cutting a lap joint in glazing bars involves a similar method to that used to cut a simple cross lap joint, but there are complications which result from joining molded sections.

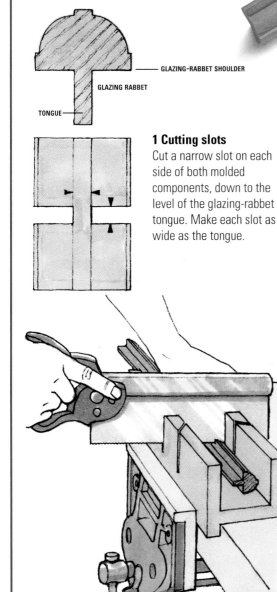

GLAZING-RABBET SHOULDER

GLAZING RABBET

TONGUE

1 Cutting slots
Cut a narrow slot on each side of both molded components, down to the level of the glazing-rabbet tongue. Make each slot as wide as the tongue.

3 Paring the miters
Pare the waste on each side of the slots to form a 45-degree miter. Make a miter block from scrap wood to help guide the chisel blade at the required angle.

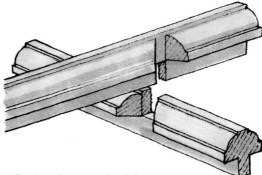

2 Using a miter box as a guide
Since it is difficult to mark a molded section, it pays to hold the work in a miter box, using the 90-degree guides when sawing the slots.

4 Cutting the cross lap joint
All that remains is to cut recesses in each component to form the actual lap joint. Cut the recesses down to the level of the glazing-rabbet shoulder.

OBLIQUE LAP JOINT
HAND CUT

The oblique lap joint is identical to the right-angle version, except for the fact that the recesses are set at an angle. Use a miter square to mark out a 45-degree joint or a sliding bevel for other angles.

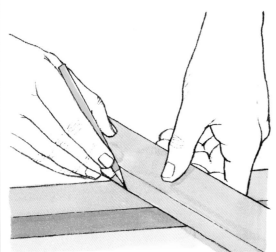

1 Marking the shoulders
Score one shoulder line across one component and, placing the second piece of wood against the line, mark its width with a pencil. Score the line with a square and marking knife. Mark the other component similarly.

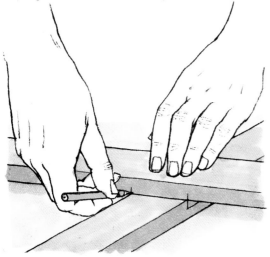

2 Marking the width of the recess
Mark the width of each recess, then use a try square to continue the shoulder lines down each edge. Scribe a line between them with a marking gauge set to half the wood's thickness.

3 Cutting the joint
Saw and chisel out the waste as described for a right-angle cross lap joint (see page 56).

USING A TABLE SAW
Cut an oblique lap joint on a table saw as described on page 56, but set the miter fence at an angle. Hold the work firmly against the fence to prevent it being drawn backwards by the saw blade.

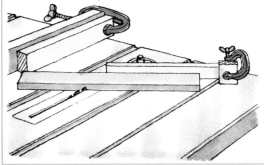

CORNER LAP JOINT
HAND CUT

You can construct a simple framework with lap joints at each corner, but since the joint relies almost entirely on the glue for strength, you may need to reinforce it with screws or dowels. Cut the joint by hand, using the method described below, or cut it on a power saw (see page 60). The mitered lap joint is a refined version, but with even less gluing area.

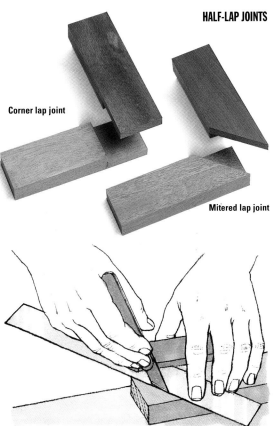

Corner lap joint

Mitered lap joint

1 Marking the basic lap joint
Lay the components side-by-side, and mark the shoulder line across both of them. Continue the lines down each edge.

1 Marking a mitered corner
Mark and cut one component as described left, then cut the lap to 45 degrees. Score the angled shoulder line across the face of the second component, using a knife and miter square, then scribe the center line up the inner edge and across the end grain.

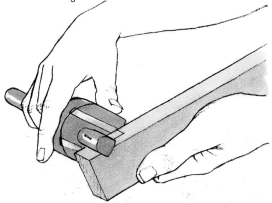

2 Gauging the depth
Set a marking gauge to half the thickness of the wood and scribe a line up both edges and across the end grain. Remove the waste with a tenon saw, cutting downwards from the end grain, followed by sawing across the shoulder.

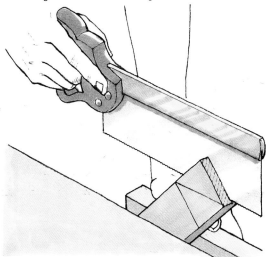

2 Cutting the angled shoulder
Clamp the work at an angle in a vise and saw on the waste side of the center line, down to the shoulder. Lay the work on a bench hook, and remove the waste by sawing down the shoulder line.

T-LAP JOINT
HAND CUT

A means of joining an intermediate support to a frame, the T-lap joint is a combination of the cross-lap and corner-lap versions.

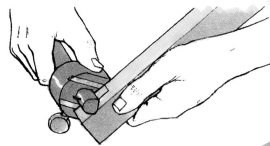

1 Marking out the joint
Taking the dimensions from the relevant components, score the shoulder lines with a knife and try square, and scribe the depth of the joint on each workpiece with a marking gauge.

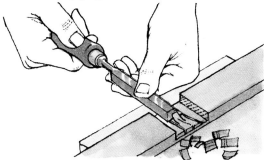

2 Cutting the recess
Chisel out the waste from between the shoulders. Use the long edge of the chisel blade to check that the bottom of the recess is flat.

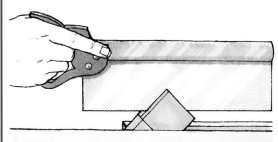

3 Sawing the lap
Saw down to the shoulder, keeping the saw blade just to the waste side of the gauged line. You may find it easier to keep the cut vertical if you tilt the work away from you while sawing down one edge. Turn the work round and saw down the other edge, then finish off by sawing squarely down to the shoulder. Saw the shoulder line to remove the waste.

USING A RADIAL-ARM SAW
The radial-arm saw is an excellent machine for cutting lap joints, since you can clearly see the shoulder lines you are sawing. Using a dado head removes more waste wood at one pass than a standard setup.

Adjust the blade to cut halfway through the work, and pull the saw towards you to cut the shoulder. Slide the work to one side, gradually removing more waste with each pass.

Clamp an end stop to the fence to cut a shoulder in the same place on identical workpieces. When cutting recesses for cross lap or T-lap joints, clamp a block at both ends of the fence.

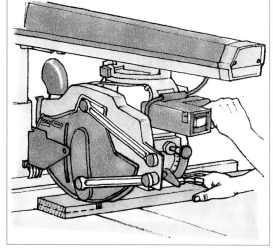

T-LAP JOINT
MACHINE CUT

A table saw or radial-arm saw is capable of producing accurate, but not particularly well-finished, lap joints. Using a router to cut the joint makes very crisp shoulders and perfectly flat surfaces. If you intend to make a number of joints, use a couple of simple jigs to guide the router.

MAKING THE JIGS

Make a pair of identical L-shape jigs by gluing and screwing together 300mm (1ft) lengths of 75 x 18mm (3 x ¾in) and 150 x 18mm (6 x ¾in) prepared wood.

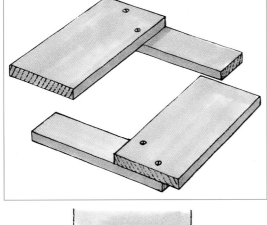

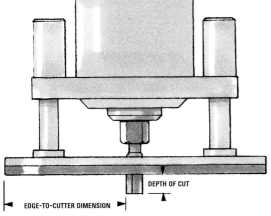

Setting up the router
Set the depth of cut on the router to half the thickness of the workpieces. Measure from the edge of the base to the side of the cutter – use this edge-to-cutter dimension to position the jigs on the work.

DOVETAIL LAP JOINT
HAND CUT

Incorporate a dovetail to increase the strength of
a T-lap joint. It is only marginally more difficult to
make than the standard square-shoulder joint.

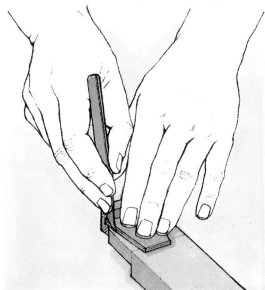

1 Marking the lap dovetail
Having marked out and cut a lap in the conventional
manner (see page 60), use a template and knife to mark
the dovetail on the workpiece.

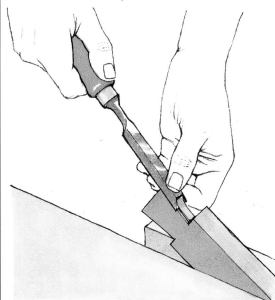

2 Shaping the lap dovetail
Saw the short shoulders on both sides of the lap, then
pare away the waste with a chisel to form the sloping
sides of the dovetail.

3 Marking and cutting the recess
Using the dovetailed lap as a template, score the
shoulders of the recess on the cross member. Mark
the depth of the recess with a marking gauge (see
page 56), and then remove the waste wood with a
tenon saw and chisel.

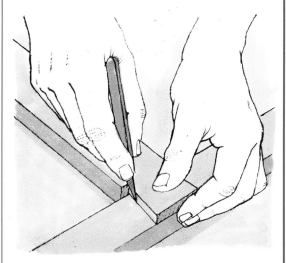

MAKING A TEMPLATE
*Cut a tapered plywood
tongue, with one side
angled for marking dovetails
in softwood and the other
for dovetailing hardwoods
(see page 82). Glue the
tongue into a slot cut in a
hardwood stock.*

CHAPTER 9 The mortise-and-tenon joint has a venerable history; it has been used for centuries to construct framed cabinets, chairs and tables. In its simplest form, the tenon, a tongue cut on the end of a rail, fits into a slot, the mortise, that is cut into a stile or leg. The basic construction has been developed and refined by generations of joiners and cabinetmakers, creating a variety of strong joints to suit different situations.

MORTISE & TENONS

THROUGH MORTISE AND TENON
HAND CUT

The through joint, where the tenon passes right through the leg, is used a great deal for constructional frames of all kinds. With the end grain showing, possibly with wooden wedges used to spread the tenon (see page 72), it is an attractive, business-like joint. Always cut the mortise first, since it is easier to make the tenon fit exactly than the other way round.

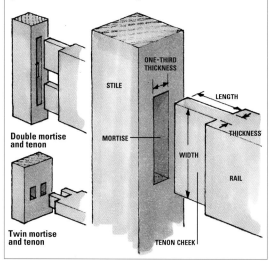

RAIL

LEG OR STILE

1 Marking the length of the mortise
Mark the position and length of the mortise, using the rail as a template. Square the lines all round with a pencil.

2 Scribing the mortise
Set a mortise gauge to match the width of the mortise chisel to be used, and then scribe the mortise centrally between the squared lines on both of its edges.

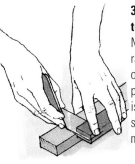

3 Marking the tenon shoulders
Mark the shoulders on the rail, allowing for slightly overlong tenons that can be planed flush when the joint is complete. Score the shoulder lines with a marking knife.

4 Scribing the tenon
Without adjusting the settings, use the mortise gauge to scribe the tenon on both edges and across the end of the rail.

PROPORTIONS OF A MORTISE AND TENON

Cut the tenon for a standard joint to approximately one-third the thickness of the rail, the exact size being determined by the chisel used to cut the mortise. Tenon thickness can be increased when the leg or mortise member is thicker than the rail.

A tenon normally runs the full width of the rail but, should the rail be unusually wide, it is best to incorporate a pair of tenons, one above the other, to avoid weakening the leg with an excessively long mortise. This type of joint is known as a double mortise and tenon. Twin tenons, cut side by side, are required when a rail is set horizontally.

Make the depth of a stopped mortise about three-quarters the width of the leg or stile.

ONE-THIRD THICKNESS

STILE

LENGTH

THICKNESS

MORTISE

WIDTH

RAIL

Double mortise and tenon

Twin mortise and tenon

TENON CHEEK

5 Chopping the mortise

Clamp the work to a bench so that you can stand at one end of the stile. Holding the chisel vertically, drive it 3 to 6mm (⅛ to ¼in) into the wood at the center of the marked mortise. Work backwards in short stages, making similar cuts and ensuring you stop about 2mm (1⁄16in) from the end of the mortise.

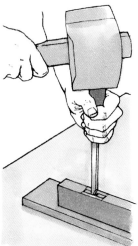

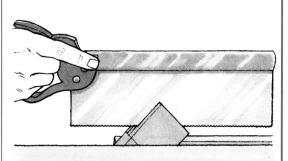

8 Sawing the tenon

Clamp the rail in a vise, set at an angle so that the end grain faces away from you. Saw down to the shoulder on the waste side of each scribed line. Turn the work around and saw down to the shoulder line on the other side of the tenon.

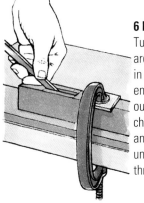

6 Removing the waste

Turn the mortise chisel around and chop the wood in stages towards the other end of the mortise. Lever out the waste with the chisel, then chop out another section of wood until you have cut halfway through the stile.

9 Cutting square

Clamp the work upright and saw parallel to the shoulder on both sides of the tenon, taking care not to overrun the marks.

7 Completing the mortise

Pare the ends of the mortise square, then turn the work over and, after shaking out any loose wood chips, clamp the stile down again so that you can chop out the waste from the other side of the joint.

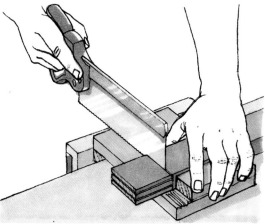

10 Sawing the shoulders

Holding the rail on a bench hook, remove the waste by sawing down the shoulder line on each side of the tenon. If necessary, pare the sides of the tenon with a chisel until it fits the mortise snugly.

DOUBLE MORTISE AND TENON
HAND CUT

A double mortise and tenon is typically used for the lock rail of a large frame-and-panel door. The gap between the tenons should be no more than one-third the width of the rail. To help prevent the rail warping, leave a short stub of wood, known as a haunch (see page 70), between the tenons.

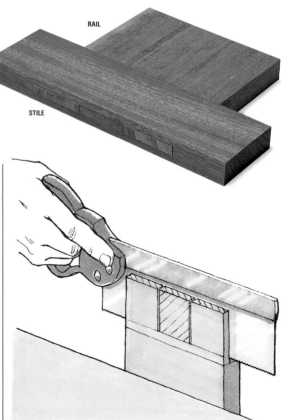

RAIL

STILE

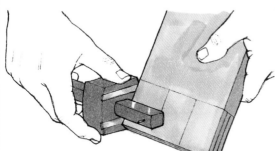

1 Marking out the tenons
Mark the shoulders and scribe the tenons as described for a standard through joint. Set a marking gauge to scribe the inner edge of both tenons on each side of the rail and across the end grain.

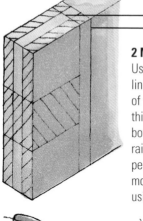

HAUNCH LINE
SHOULDER LINE

2 Marking the haunch
Using a try square, pencil a line representing the length of the haunch (equal to the thickness of the tenon) on both sides and edges of the rail. Mark the waste with a pencil. Mark out the mortises (see page 64), using the rail as a template.

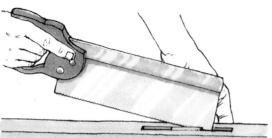

3 Cutting the mortises
Chop out both mortises as described on page 65, then run a saw blade alongside the haunch lines gauged between them. Chisel out the waste between the saw cuts, down to the level of the haunch.

4 Sawing the tenons
Clamp the rail upright and, standing at the side of the rail, first saw down the inner edge of each tenon, stopping at the haunch line. Change your position to saw alongside both tenons, all the way down to the shoulder lines.

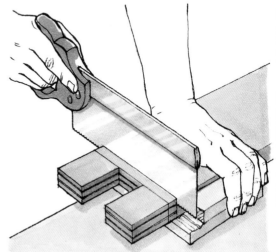

5 Removing the waste
Cut out the wood from between the tenons, using a coping saw, then saw the shoulder on each side of the joint to remove what is left of the waste.

TWIN MORTISE AND TENON
HAND CUT

The twin mortise and tenon is used when a rail, turned on its side, is jointed into the face of a leg rather than its edge. It is also commonly used for drawer-rail construction. Depending on the section of the rail, there may be a pair of tenons cut to standard proportions, or two relatively thick pin tenons (see page 68). As a rule, make each tenon as thick as the gap between them.

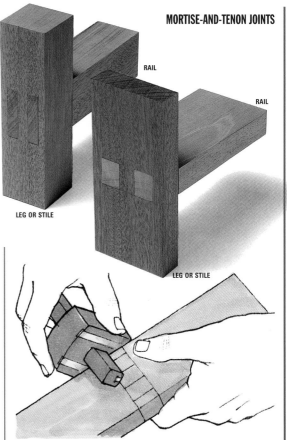

RAIL

RAIL

LEG OR STILE

LEG OR STILE

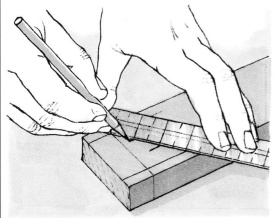

1 Marking out tenon thickness
Having squared the shoulder lines all round, make a pencil mark not less than 6mm (¼in) from each edge, then divide the space between into three, to give a pair of tenons and the gap between them. Modify the thickness of the tenons to match a suitable chisel.

3 Marking out the mortises
Square two lines across the work to mark the top and bottom of the mortises, then scribe lines between them to mark the sides of the mortises, using the marking gauge. If the mortises are to be cut into a wider rail or panel, leave the pin settings alone but adjust the tool's stock to mark both mortises from one edge.

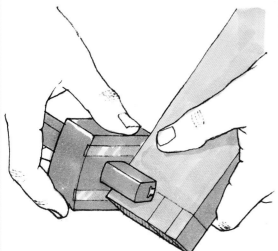

2 Scribing the tenons
Set a mortise gauge to the above dimensions, and scribe the tenons on both faces and across the end of the rail, working from both edges.

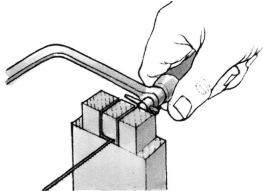

4 Cutting the joint
Chop out the mortises as described on page 65. Saw down beside each tenon, following the scribed lines, then cut off the waste wood from both edges of the rail by sawing along the shoulder lines. Remove the waste from between the tenons with a coping saw and chisel (see also page 68).

PINNED MORTISE AND TENON
HAND CUT

A pinned version of the joint comprises a row of
evenly spaced, stubby tenons (pins) for fitting
wide, fixed shelves or partitions into a cabinet.
When the tenons pass right through the panel, they
are usually held firmly in place with hardwood
wedges set into sawcuts made across the end grain
of each pin. For decorative reasons, the wedges
are sometimes set diagonally.

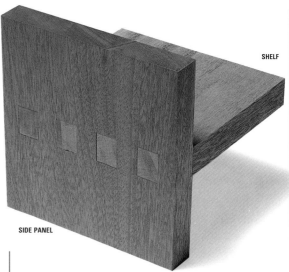

SHELF

SIDE PANEL

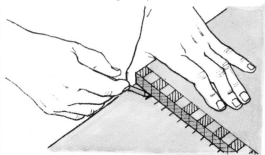

1 Marking out the joint
Mark out the shelf as described for a twin mortise and
tenon (see page 67), dividing the shoulder line with a
row of evenly spaced pins. Modify the size of the pins
to match your chisel. Mark the positions of the
mortises, using the shelf as a template.

2 Cutting the mortises
Chop out the through
mortises (see page 65),
working from both sides
of the panel.

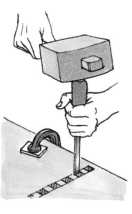

3 Cutting the pins
Saw down the sides of the
pins with a tenon saw, then
remove the waste from
between them with a
coping saw. Trim the
shoulders with a chisel.

4 Wedging the pins
Make a diagonal saw cut across the end of each pin,
down to the shoulder line. Having glued and assembled
the joint, drive in glued wedges and leave to set before
planing them flush with the panel.

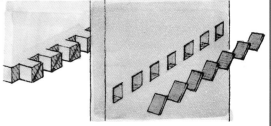

STOPPED-DADO VERSION
*Make an even stronger version of this joint by
incorporating a stopped dado that houses the pinned
end of the shelf. This joint is normally made with
stopped pins. Cut the dado first. Allow for the depth
of the dado when marking the shoulder line for the
pins on the end of the shelf. When you have cut them,
saw a notch out of the front edge of the shelf to
accommodate the stopped end of the dado.*

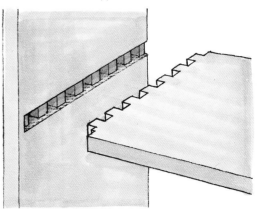

STOPPED MORTISE AND TENON
HAND CUT

The majority of tables and chairs are made with stopped mortise-and-tenon joints, with no obvious signs of the joint on the outside of the leg. It is a good-looking joint that is no more difficult to make than a through tenon, once you have learned how to accurately gauge the depth of the mortise.

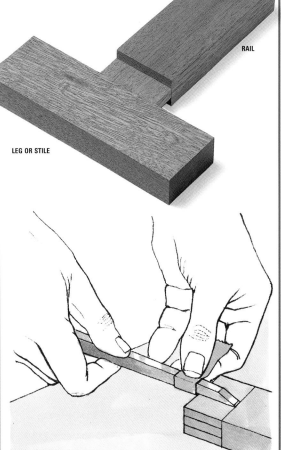

RAIL

LEG OR STILE

1 Marking out the tenon
Score the shoulder line all round the rail (see page 64 for proportions), and scribe the thickness of the tenon with a mortise gauge.

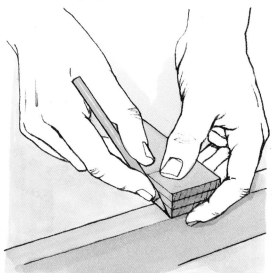

2 Marking out the mortise
Use the rail as a guide for marking out the mortise position on the leg or stile. Square the lines across the edge of the work, and use the same gauge to scribe the mortise between them.

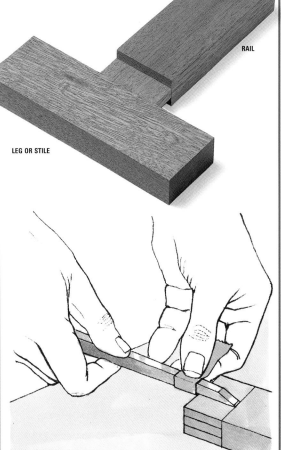

3 Making a depth gauge
To gauge the depth of the mortise, lay the blade of the chisel on the marked rail, with its cutting edge aligned with the shoulder line. Wrap adhesive tape around the blade at a point just beyond the end of the rail.

4 Cutting the joint
Cutting into one edge of the rail, chop out the mortise as described on page 65, stopping when the tape wrapped around the blade is level with the surface of the wood. Saw the tenon to match.

HAUNCHED MORTISE AND TENON
HAND CUT

In order to include a strong joint at the corner of a frame, it is essential to offset the tenon slightly, to prevent it breaking through the end grain of the leg or stile. To support the top edge of the rail, a small integral tongue, known as a haunch, fits into a shallow groove cut just above the mortise. Cut a sloping haunch if you want it to be invisible when the joint is assembled.

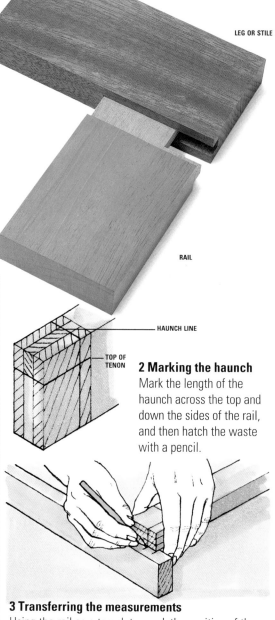

LEG OR STILE

RAIL

PROPORTIONS OF A HAUNCHED TENON

Make the tenon two-thirds the width of the rail; the haunch itself should be as long as it is thick. Make a sloping haunch to the same proportions, but pare it away to meet the shoulder line.

EQUAL EQUAL

TWO-THIRDS WIDTH

Square haunch

EQUAL EQUAL

TWO-THIRDS WIDTH

Sloping haunch

HAUNCH LINE

TOP OF TENON

2 Marking the haunch
Mark the length of the haunch across the top and down the sides of the rail, and then hatch the waste with a pencil.

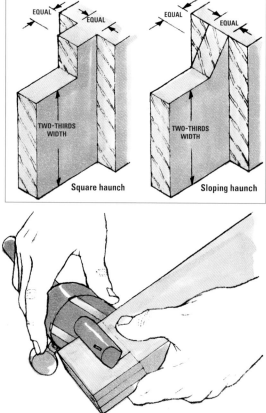

3 Transferring the measurements
Using the rail as a template, mark the position of the mortise on the stile. At this stage, let the end of the stile project by about 18mm (¾in) to prevent splitting. This extension, known as the horn, is cut off and planed flush when the joint is complete.

1 Marking out the tenon
Having marked the shoulders and scribed the tenon thickness on the rail (see page 64), use a marking gauge to scribe the top edge of the tenon on both sides and across the end grain.

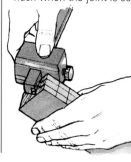

4 Scribing the mortise
Scribe the mortise up to the end of the stile, and then continue the lines a short way onto the end grain; this marks the end of the haunch groove.

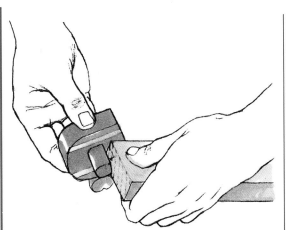

5 Marking the depth of the groove
Scribe a short line on the end of the stile to mark the depth of the haunch groove.

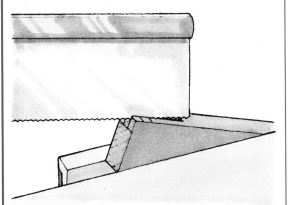

6 Cutting the mortise
Having cut the mortise (see page 65), extend the sides by sawing along the gauged lines, down to the bottom of the haunch groove.

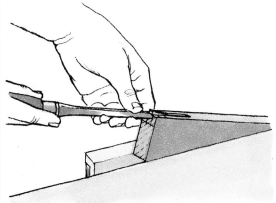

7 Paring the groove
Use a chisel to pare away the waste, leaving the bottom of the groove square.

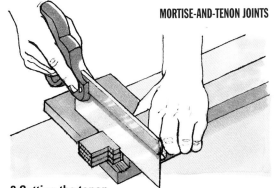

8 Cutting the tenon
After sawing the sides of the tenon (see page 65), clamp the work upright in a vise and saw beside the line marking the top edge of the tenon, down to the haunch. Reposition the work and saw down the end of the haunch, forming a notch at the top corner of the joint. Finally, saw along the shoulders to remove waste from both sides of the tenon.

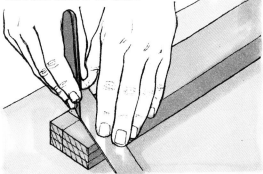

1 Making a sloping haunch
Mark out the tenon, including the haunch (see opposite), then score the sloping sides of the haunch with a marking knife. Saw down this line, after first cutting along the top edge of the tenon (see above).

2 Trimming the mortise
When marking out the mortise, continue the gauged lines up to the top of the stile, but not over the end. Having chopped out the mortise, saw the sides of the haunch groove at an angle, taking care not to overrun, then pare the slope with a chisel.

WEDGED MORTISE AND TENON
HAND CUT

A well-made mortise and tenon is normally strong enough to hold the joint together using glue alone. However, if a joint has to resist more than average leverage, expand the tenon dovetail-fashion with hardwood wedges. You can wedge both through and stopped tenons – when hidden, they are known as fox wedges.

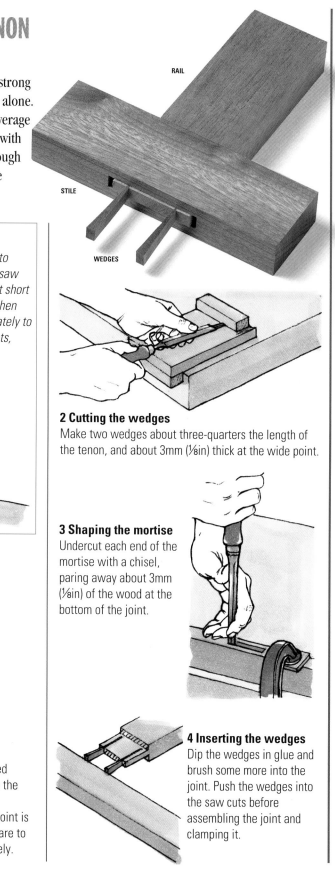

RAIL

STILE

WEDGES

WEDGING THROUGH TENONS

Cut a shallow slope at each end of the mortise to allow room for the tenon to expand. Make two saw cuts down the length of the tenon, stopping just short of the shoulders. Glue and assemble the joint, then drive in the glued wedges, tapping them alternately to spread the tenon evenly. When the adhesive sets, plane end grain and wedges flush.

2 Cutting the wedges
Make two wedges about three-quarters the length of the tenon, and about 3mm (⅛in) thick at the wide point.

3 Shaping the mortise
Undercut each end of the mortise with a chisel, paring away about 3mm (⅛in) of the wood at the bottom of the joint.

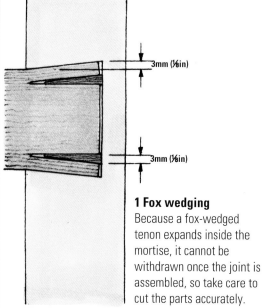

3mm (⅛in)

3mm (⅛in)

1 Fox wedging
Because a fox-wedged tenon expands inside the mortise, it cannot be withdrawn once the joint is assembled, so take care to cut the parts accurately.

4 Inserting the wedges
Dip the wedges in glue and brush some more into the joint. Push the wedges into the saw cuts before assembling the joint and clamping it.

LOOSE-WEDGED MORTISE AND TENON
HAND CUT

A loose-wedged joint must be constructed with generous shoulders and a stout tenon that will resist splitting. The wedge is normally set vertically to prevent it working loose. Since the joint is designed to be broken down, no glue is used, and it relies on the clamping force of the wedge to provide rigidity.

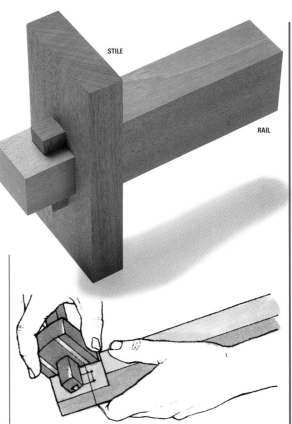

STILE

RAIL

PROPORTIONS OF A LOOSE-WEDGED JOINT

The total length of the tenon should be at least three times the thickness of the stile, and it should be not less than one-third the width of the rail. The mortise for the loose wedge should be approximately 18mm (¾in) long and about one-third of the tenon in width. The outer end of this mortise slopes to accommodate the wedge; the inner end is cut square.

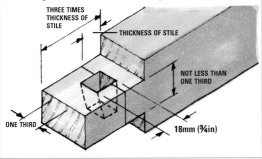

THREE TIMES THICKNESS OF STILE

THICKNESS OF STILE

NOT LESS THAN ONE THIRD

ONE THIRD

18mm (¾in)

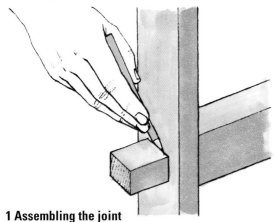

1 Assembling the joint
Cut the mortise and tenon as described on pages 64-5, but make them a sliding fit. Assemble the joint and mark the thickness of the stile on the projecting tenon.

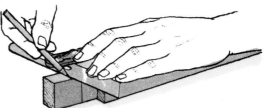

2 Marking the wedge mortise
Take the joint apart and mark the mortise for the loose wedge on the top edge of the tenon. Set the inner end of the mortise about 3mm (⅛in) inside the line marking the thickness of the stile.

3 Marking the sloping end
Set a sliding bevel to an angle of 1:6. From the line marking the outer end of the wedge mortise, draw another line on the side of the tenon, using the bevel. Square this line across the bottom of the tenon, then scribe the sides of the wedge mortise up to the line.

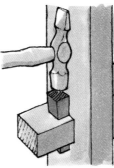

4 Completing the joint
Cut the wedge mortise, paring the sloping end with a chisel. Assemble the joint and tap in the wedge to draw the shoulders up tight.

GROOVED-FRAME MORTISE AND TENON
HAND CUT

The frame of a traditional panelled door is grooved on the inside to accommodate the panel. When haunched mortise-and-tenon joints are used at the corners, align the grooves with the mortises and make them both the same width. In addition, match the depth of the groove to the length of the haunch, so that the one neatly fills the other at the end of the stile. It is usually easier to cut the groove after the joints.

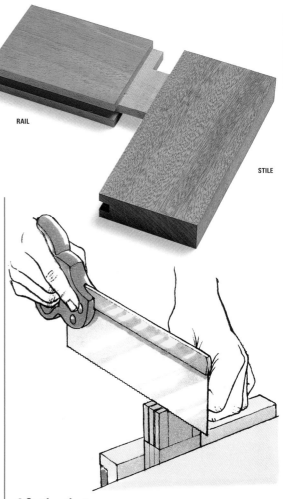

RAIL

STILE

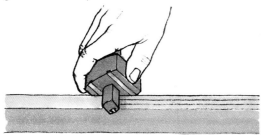

1 Scribing the panel grooves
Use a mortise gauge to scribe grooves on the inside of the rails and stiles.

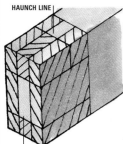

HAUNCH LINE

BOTTOM OF TENON

2 Marking out the tenon
Mark out the tenon (see page 70) then, with a marking gauge set to the depth of the groove, scribe the bottom edge of the tenon on both sides and across the end of the rail.

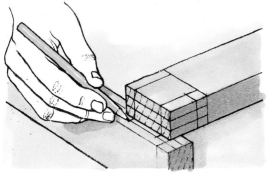

3 Transferring the measurements
Using the rail as a template, mark the position of the mortise on the stile. Cut a simple stopped mortise on these marks; cutting the panel groove at a later stage also makes room for the haunch.

4 Cutting the tenon
Cut the tenon as described on page 71, but make a second saw cut across the end of the rail to form the bottom of the tenon.

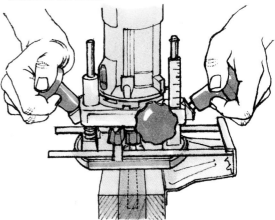

5 Cutting the panel grooves
Plane or router the grooves on the inside of the rails and stiles, then make and fit the panel before gluing and assembling the frame.

RABBETED-FRAME MORTISE AND TENON
HAND CUT

When making a glazed door for a cabinet, cut a rabbet on the inside of the rails and stiles to take the glass. Each corner of the frame can be joined with a haunched mortise and tenon, but it is necessary to stagger the shoulders in order to close off the rabbet at the end of the stile. It is probably easier to cut the rabbets after the joints. When the doorframe is complete, lay the glass in the rabbets and hold it in place with putty or a wooden bead.

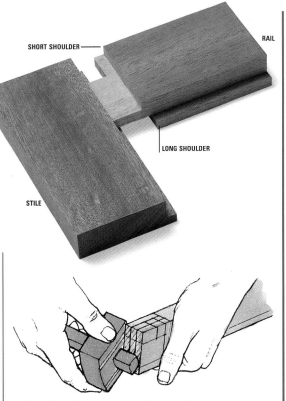

SHORT SHOULDER

RAIL

LONG SHOULDER

STILE

1 Scribing the rabbets
Set a marking gauge to one-third the thickness of the workpieces, and scribe the depth of the rabbet on the inner edge of the rails and stiles. Reset the gauge to about 6mm (¼in) and scribe the rabbet width.

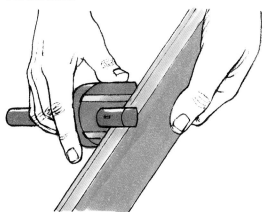

2 Marking the long shoulder
Referring to the proportions given for a standard haunched mortise and tenon (see page 70), score the long shoulder across the outer face of the rail. Using a pencil, square this line across both edges.

3 Marking the short shoulder and tenon
Mark the short shoulder across the inner face; it should be as far from the long-shoulder line as the width of the rabbet – about 6mm (¼in). Square the line across both edges. Mark out the haunch, then scribe the thickness of the tenon with a mortise gauge. Use a marking gauge to scribe the bottom of the tenon.

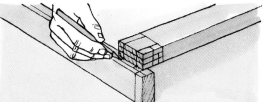

4 Marking out the mortise
Transfer the dimension from the rail to mark the position of the mortise on the stile. Gauge the thickness of the mortise. Use the same tool to mark the length of the haunch, measured from the long-shoulder line, onto the end of the stile. Hatch waste wood with a pencil.

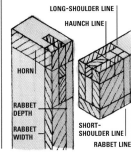

LONG-SHOULDER LINE

HAUNCH LINE

HORN

RABBET DEPTH

RABBET WIDTH

SHORT-SHOULDER LINE

RABBET LINE

5 Cutting the joints and rabbets
After cutting the joints, plane or router the rabbets on the inside of the rails and stiles. Finally, pare out the haunch waste from each joint (see page 71).

MOLDED-FRAME MORTISE AND TENON
HAND CUT

When a rabbeted frame is also molded, it is necessary to miter the ends of the moldings after the mortise and tenons have been cut. A possible alternative method is to scribe one end of the molding to cover the other; the scribing is relatively difficult, but it is better for disguising gaps if the joint should shrink.

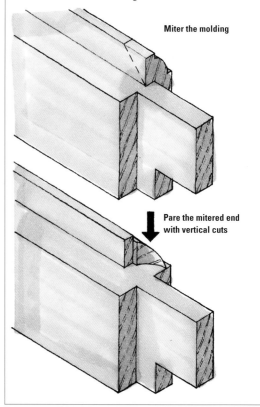

STILE

RAIL

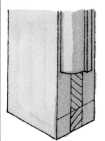

1 Trimming the molding
Before marking out the joint, cut away the molding down to the level of the rabbet, leaving a flat edge on the stile equal to the width of the tenon plus the haunch. Similarly, trim the molding off the rail, back to the shoulder line.

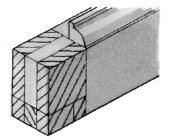

2 Marking out and cutting the joint
Mark out a haunched mortise and tenon, and cut both halves of the joint (see page 70-1).

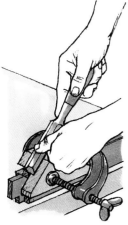

3 Mitering the molding
Trim the ends of the molded sections to 45 degrees. Clamp a guide block over the molding to keep the chisel blade at the required angle.

SCRIBING THE MOLDING

Leave the stile molding cut square as described in stage 1 (see left). Miter the end of the rail molding, then, using a gouge and straight chisel, pare away the wood on the inside of the miter until it fits around the contour of the stile molding.

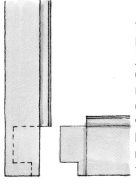

Miter the molding

Pare the mitered end with vertical cuts

CORNER MORTISE AND TENON
HAND CUT

On the majority of tables, two rails are joined to a single leg at each corner. The joints are cut as previously described, except that the ends of the tenons are mitered where they meet inside the leg. To make tapered chair frames, however, either the side-rail mortises must be cut at an angle, or the tenons are skewed to fit square-cut mortises.

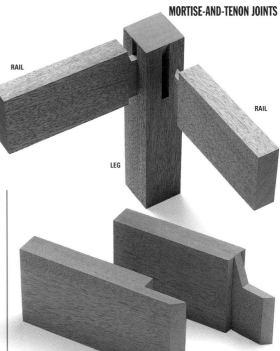

RAIL

RAIL

LEG

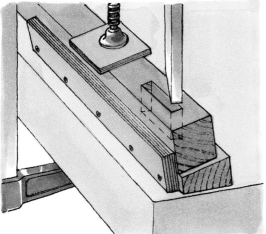

Angled mortises
A stronger joint results if you keep the tenons in line with the rails. Mark out each joint in the usual way, but mark the shoulders at an angle to fit the face of the leg. You may find it easier to cut the mortise if you make a simple jig that holds the leg at the required angle, so that you can keep your chisel blade or drill vertical when cutting the joint.

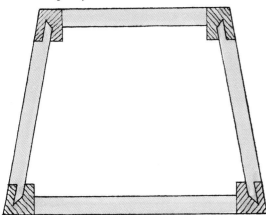

Using barefaced tenons
Design a frame with barefaced tenons if you want the rails to lie flush with the legs.

Barefaced tenon

Skewed tenon

Skewed tenons
Since it is easier to cut square mortises, it may be more convenient to skew the tenons. However, the inevitable short grain makes for relatively weak joints, so keep the angle to a minimum. It is impossible to mark skewed tenons with a mortise gauge, so use a sliding bevel and marking knife instead.

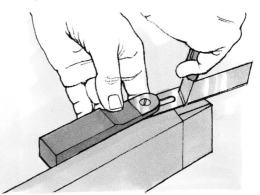

CORNER JOINTS FOR ROUND LEGS
It is easier to cut the mortises before you turn a round leg. Having cut the tenons, trim the shoulders with a gouge to fit the curve.

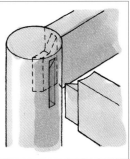

MACHINE-CUT MORTISES

If you plan to cut a number of joints, it is well worth setting up a machine tool to make your production easier and faster. A drill press (or a power drill in a bench stand) can be used to remove most of the waste before finishing the job by hand, or – better still – you can fit a special mortising attachment to the drill press.

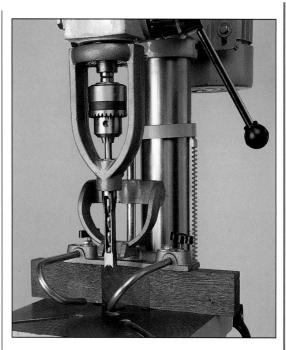

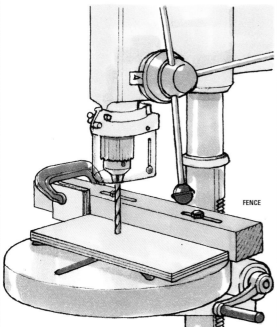

FENCE

Preparing the drill press

Clamp a wooden fence to the base of the drill press, and adjust it to center the point of the drill bit on the mortise. Set the tool's depth stop to drill to the base of a stopped mortise. Place a board beneath the work if you are drilling through mortises.

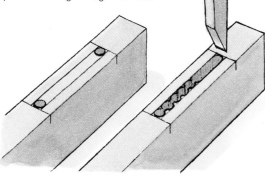

Cutting the mortise

Drill a hole at each end of the mortise, then connect them with a row of slightly overlapping holes. Pare the sides and ends square with chisels.

Using a mortising attachment

Adapt a drill press by fitting a mortising attachment, comprising an auger drill that removes the waste, coupled with a square hollow chisel which shapes the mortise at the same time.

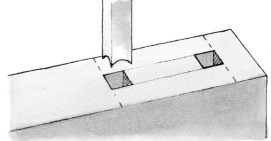

1 Cutting the ends square

Start the mortise by cutting a square hole at each end. Plunge the chisel firmly but don't force it, especially when working hardwoods.

2 Removing the waste

Remove the waste between the holes in stages. Work steadily at an even pace, to avoid any overheating of the auger bit.

Using a slot mortiser

It is possible to adapt a planer-thicknesser to machine mortises by fitting a milling chuck to the end of the tool's cutter block. The workpiece is moved relative to the stationary cutter by means of a special mortising table that is adjustable in height. When using this type of attachment, it is imperative to cover the planer cutters with the appropriate guard.

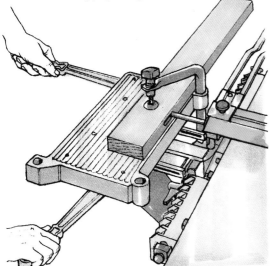

Cutting a mortise

Avoid the risk of breaking the cutter by machining a mortise in stages, and never plunge deeper than the cutter's diameter during any one pass. Since the machined mortise has rounded ends, either chop them square with a chisel or file the corners off the tenon.

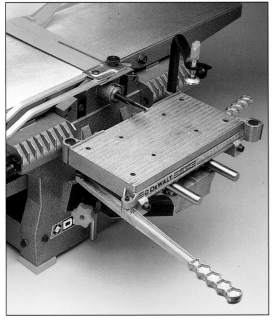

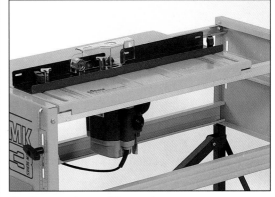

Cutting mortises with a router

Although you can cut mortises with a hand-held router, it is much more convenient to machine them with the tool inverted in a router table or workcenter. Once you have made the initial adjustments, you can cut any number of identical mortises without having to mark out the workpieces.

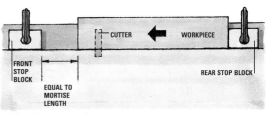

1 Setting up end stops

With all the workpieces cut to size, clamp a block of wood at each end of the fence to limit the movement of a workpiece to the length of the required mortise.

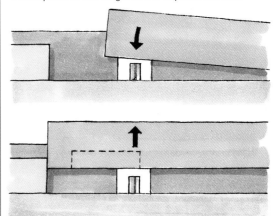

2 Machining the mortise

With the work butted against the rear end stop, hold the wood firmly against the fence and lower it slowly onto the rotating cutter. Feed the wood forward until it comes to rest against the other end stop, then carefully lift it clear of the cutter. Cut a deep mortise in stages, raising the cutter between each pass.

MACHINE-CUT TENONS

Although it is largely a matter of personal choice, perhaps the best way to produce tenons in quantity is to use a table saw. You can work relatively quickly without damaging its blade or powerful motor, and the sharp carbide-tipped saw teeth cut so cleanly that there should be no need for final fitting by hand. It may be possible to buy a purpose-made tenon-cutting jig for a particular model of saw; such jigs are designed to slide along the slot machined across the saw table for the miter fence. Alternatively, you can make your own jig from MDF.

Making a tenon-cutting jig
Cut the components from 12 to 18mm (½ to ¾in) MDF to fit your saw table. Make the slide from a metal strip that is an accurate sliding fit in the miter-fence slot. Before machining joints, always make a test component and use it to check your settings before proceeding with actual workpieces.

1 Cutting the tenon cheeks
Clamp the work to the jig and feed it past the blade to cut along one side of the tenon. Turn the work round and saw the other side.

2 Sawing the shoulders
Crosscut the joint's shoulders, using the miter fence to feed the work past the blade. A block of wood clamped to the saw's rip fence serves to align the shoulder with the blade and also prevents the severed waste jamming between the blade and fence.

Cutting a haunch
Adjust the rip fence until the blade aligns with the end of the haunch. Make the first cut and remove the waste in stages, sliding the workpiece away sideways from the rip fence.

CUTTING TENONS ON A RADIAL-ARM SAW
With the workpiece butted against an end stop clamped to the fence, make the first cut along the shoulder line. Slide the work sideways, removing the waste little by little with successive crosscuts. Turn the work over and repeat the procedure to cut the other side of the tenon.

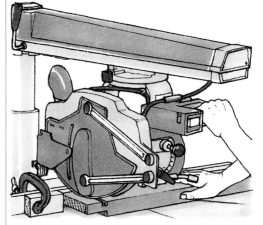

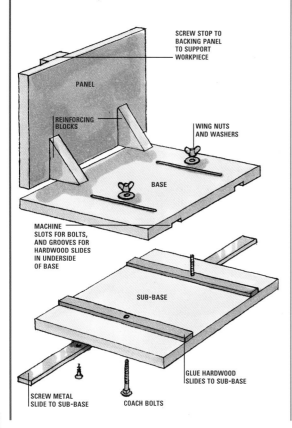

SCREW STOP TO
BACKING PANEL
TO SUPPORT
WORKPIECE

PANEL

REINFORCING
BLOCKS

WING NUTS
AND WASHERS

BASE

MACHINE
SLOTS FOR BOLTS,
AND GROOVES FOR
HARDWOOD SLIDES
IN UNDERSIDE
OF BASE

SUB-BASE

GLUE HARDWOOD
SLIDES TO SUB-BASE

SCREW METAL
SLIDE TO SUB-BASE

COACH BOLTS

CHAPTER *10* Traditional drawer making utilizes the inherent strength of the dovetail joint to full advantage: the fan-shape 'tails' resist the forces applied to the joints when the drawer is used. Dovetails are so strong that it is rare to see a drawer that has broken as a result of joint failure, even when heavily laden. There is a great variety of forms of dovetail joints, some of which are used primarily for their decorative qualities.

DOVETAIL JOINTS

THROUGH DOVETAIL JOINT
HAND CUT

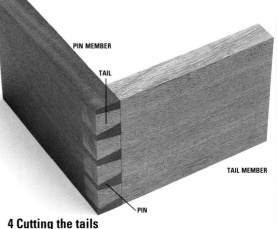

PIN MEMBER

TAIL

TAIL MEMBER

PIN

The ability to cut tight-fitting dovetail joints seems to be regarded as the ultimate test of the woodworker's skill. It is also, undeniably, one of the most efficient joints for constructing boxes and cabinets from solid wood. Through dovetails, the most basic form of the joint, are visible on both sides of a corner.

1 Scribing the shoulder line
Plane square the ends of both workpieces and, with a cutting gauge set to the thickness of the pin member, scribe the shoulder line for the tails on all sides of the other workpiece.

2 Spacing the tails
A good hand-cut joint has equal-size tails matched with relatively narrow pins. Pencil a line across the end grain, 6mm (¼in) from each edge of the work, then divide the distance between the lines equally, depending on the required number of tails. Measure 3mm (⅛in) on each side of these marks and square pencil lines across the end.

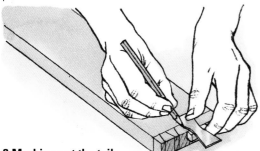

3 Marking out the tails
Mark the sloping sides of each tail on the face side of the workpiece, using an adjustable bevel or a ready-made dovetail template. Mark the waste with a pencil.

4 Cutting the tails
Clamp the work at an angle in a vise so that you can saw vertically beside each dovetail. When you have reached the last tail in the row, cant the work in the other direction and saw down the other side of each tail.

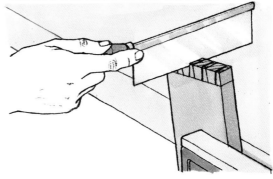

DOVETAIL ANGLES
The sides of a dovetail must slope at the optimum angle. An exaggerated slope results in weak short grain at the tips of the dovetail, while insufficient taper invariably leads to a slack joint. Ideally, mark a 1:8 angle for hardwoods, but increase the angle to 1:6 for softwoods. The proportion of each tail is a matter of personal interpretation, but a row of small, regularly spaced tails looks better than a few large ones, and also makes for a stronger joint.

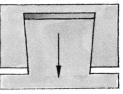

Exaggerated slope

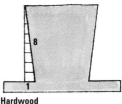

Insufficient taper

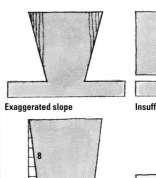

Hardwood

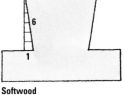

Softwood

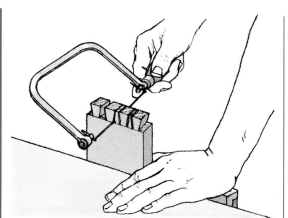

5 Removing the waste
Set the work horizontally in the vise so that you can remove the corner waste with the dovetail saw, then cut the waste from between the tails, this time using a coping saw.

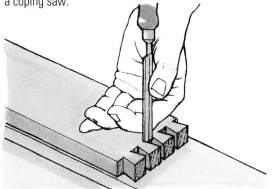

6 Trimming the shoulders
Use a bevel-edge chisel to trim what remains of the waste from between the tails. Finish flush with the shoulder line.

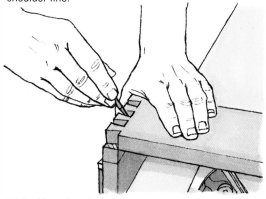

7 Marking the pins
Set the cutting gauge to the thickness of the tail member and scribe shoulder lines for the pins on the other component. Coat its end grain with chalk and clamp it upright in a vise. Position the cut tails precisely on the end of the workpiece, then mark their shape in the chalk with a pointed scriber or knife.

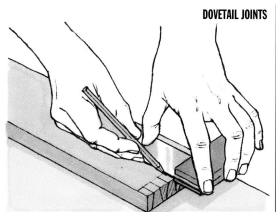

8 Marking cutting lines
Align a try square with the marks scored in the chalk, and draw parallel lines down to the shoulder on both sides of the work. Hatch the waste between the pins with a pencil.

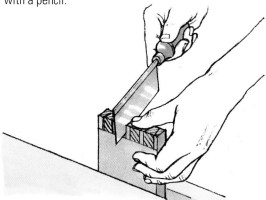

9 Cutting the pins
Make fine saw cuts on both sides of each pin, following the angled lines marked across the chalked end grain. Finish flush with the shoulder.

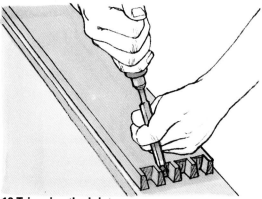

10 Trimming the joint
Remove most of the waste wood with a coping saw, and pare the shoulders with a chisel. Assemble the joint dry, trimming any tight spots until the joint fits cleanly and snugly.

THROUGH DOVETAIL JOINT
MACHINE CUT

The versatility of the router has been enhanced by the development of ingenious jigs for cutting traditional joints. Although the initial adjustment is time-consuming, once these jigs are set, even complicated dovetail joints can be cut in a fraction of the time it takes to make them by hand.

The description here serves as a guide to cutting through dovetails on a jig that features individually adjustable fingers that guide the router cutter. The setting of the finger assembly governs the size and spacing of the tails and pins. Adjusting the fingers for the pins along one side of the assembly automatically sets the fingers for matching tails on the opposite side. There is also a device for fine fore-and-aft adjustment of the finger assembly.

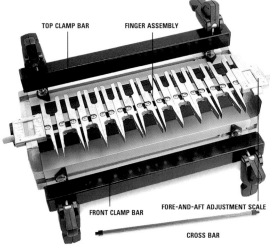

TOP CLAMP BAR   FINGER ASSEMBLY

FRONT CLAMP BAR   FORE-AND-AFT ADJUSTMENT SCALE

CROSS BAR

Fitting a test piece
Use test pieces to set up the jig and check the fit of the parts. Place an 18mm (¾in) spacer board under the finger assembly and secure it with the jig's top clamp bar. Clamp a test piece of the correct width to the front of the jig, making sure it butts against the side stop and the underside of the finger assembly.

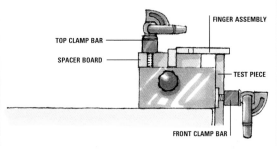

FINGER ASSEMBLY

TOP CLAMP BAR

SPACER BOARD

TEST PIECE

FRONT CLAMP BAR

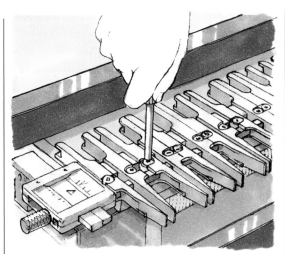

Adjusting the finger assembly
You need one pair of fingers for each dovetail and a single finger at both ends of the row. Set these individual fingers first so that they are flush with each edge of the test piece, then space the pairs of fingers at regular intervals between them. Tighten the clamping screws.

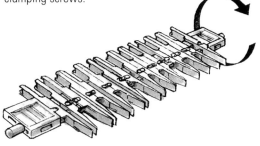

Rotating the fingers
Once you have adjusted one half of the assembly, all that is required to utilize the other set of fingers is to unclamp the entire assembly, rotate it, and clamp it down again.

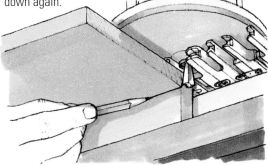

1 Setting up for tail cutting
Set the assembly with the straight-sided tail fingers pointing towards you. Fit into the router a compatible dovetail cutter and guide bush – check with your jig supplier. Using the other component as a template, mark the depth of cut on the tail member, and adjust the router cutter down to the marked line.

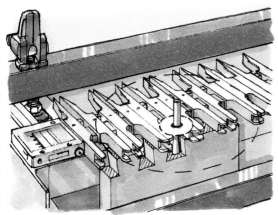

2 Cutting the tails

Always check that all parts of the jig and the test piece are securely clamped before switching on the router. Then run the cutter between each set of fingers (see box, right), cutting out the waste wood which leaves a neat row of tails.

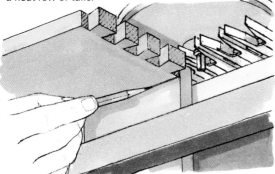

3 Setting up for pin cutting

Rotate the assembly to present the pin fingers to the front of the jig, and clamp a second test piece in the jig. Mark the depth of cut as before, using the tail member you have just cut as a template. Fit a straight cutter in the router and adjust it down to the marked line.

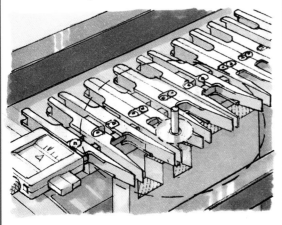

4 Cutting the pins

With the router placed flat on the finger assembly, switch on and then rout out the waste between each pair of fingers.

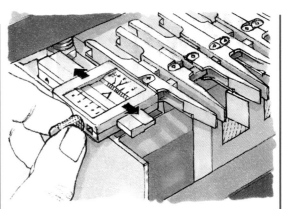

5 Checking the fit

Assemble the joint to check it fits snugly. If it is slack, use the jig's fine-adjustment scale to move the finger assembly forward. If the joint is too tight, adjust the finger assembly backwards. Cut another pair of test pieces to check that the joint fits satisfactorily, before proceeding with the actual workpieces.

CUTTING NEAT PIN AND TAIL SOCKETS

Simply driving the router cutter straight through the workpiece tears out the wood fibers along the shoulder line. Using the following sequence, incorporating a technique known as 'back cutting', takes a little longer but leaves you with neat sockets.

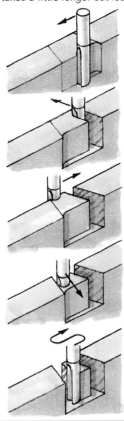

1 Make a shallow cut in the face of the wood, guiding the machine from right to left (back cutting).

2 Return to the right of the socket and feed the cutter through to the back of the workpiece.

3 Make another shallow cut across the back of the socket.

4 Feed the cutter towards you on the left-hand side.

5 Remove the waste from the center of the socket.

DECORATIVE THROUGH DOVETAIL JOINT
HAND CUT

A standard through dovetail is considered to be attractive, and the decorative qualities of the joint can be exploited still further by varying the size and spacing of the tails and pins. The example shown here has fine triangular pins and a central half-depth dovetail that interrupts the regular rhythm of the joint.

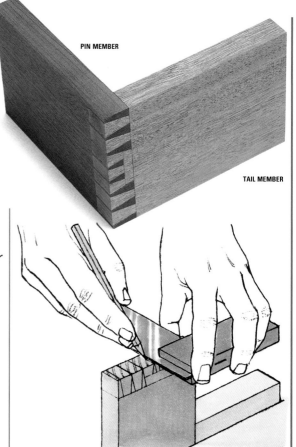

PIN MEMBER

TAIL MEMBER

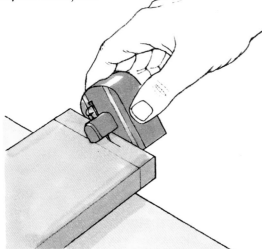

1 Scribing the shoulder line
Begin by marking out the tails, lightly scribing the shoulder line on all sides of the workpiece. Similarly mark the shoulder line for the half-depth dovetail.

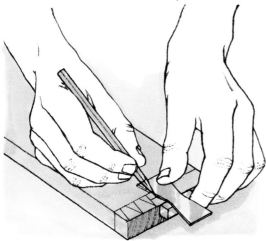

2 Marking the sloping sides
Use a dovetail template to draw the sloping sides of the tails. Group the tails closely together, with no more than the thickness of a saw cut between them.

3 Squaring across the end grain
Using a try square, draw the tips of the tails on the end of the workpiece, then, with a dovetail saw and coping saw, remove the waste between them as described for a standard through dovetail joint. Trim the shoulder lines square with a narrow bevel-edge chisel.

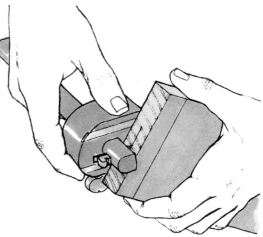

4 Scribing the pin shoulder line
Mark the shoulder line on all four sides of the pin member, then reset the gauge to score the length of the half-depth pins on the end grain. Rub chalk on the end of the workpiece.

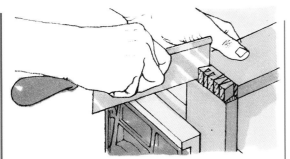

5 Marking the pins

With the tail member held down on the end of the pin member, score the shape of the pins in the chalk by drawing the tip of a dovetail saw between each pair of tails. Square the marks down to the shoulder line on both sides, and then hatch the waste, using a pencil.

6 Cutting the pins

Cut out the waste from between the pins, using a dovetail saw and coping saw, then pare down to the shoulder line with a chisel. To trim the half-depth pins to size, first make a cut across the grain close to the shoulder line, using a chisel and mallet.

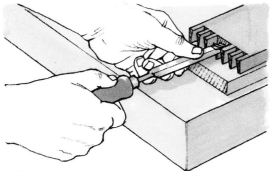

7 Paring away the waste

Cutting towards the shoulder, pare the pins down to the line scribed on the end grain. Finally, cut across the grain once more to trim accurately to the shoulder line.

ROUTING DECORATIVE DOVETAILS

Using a dovetail jig with adjustable fingers, it is possible to cut decorative joints with a power router. You need two different dovetail cutters and a straight cutter, all with suitable guide bushes.

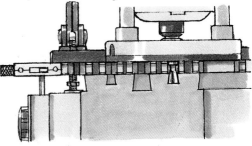

1 Making the tails

Set up the jig and adjust the fingers (see pages 84-5). Make trial cuts to ascertain the exact finger settings required for each dovetail cutter. Clamp the work in the jig, machine the larger pin sockets, then swap cutters and machine the smaller ones.

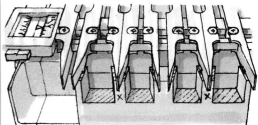

2 Making the pins

Since some of the pins are narrower than others, you must experiment with fore-and-aft adjustment of the finger assembly until you achieve the appropriate settings for cutting each size of pin. Make a careful note of these settings for reference. Cut all the sockets with the straight cutter, then adjust the finger assembly backwards so that you can shave the narrow pins down to size.

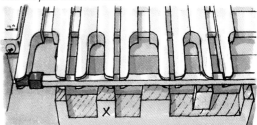

3 Shortening the pins

Turn the pin member to face inwards and rotate the finger assembly. Fit the jig's crossbar attachment to the fingers and adjust the assembly backwards, so that you can feed the router along the bar to shorten the narrow pins.

MITERED THROUGH DOVETAIL
HAND CUT

Should you wish to mold the edge of a dovetailed workpiece, perhaps to make a sliding tray or an open box, incorporate a miter at each corner.

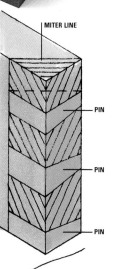

TAIL MEMBER

PIN MEMBER

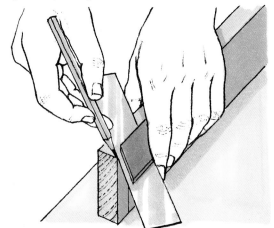

1 Marking the tail member
After scribing the shoulder line on the two sides and across the bottom of the tail member, mark the miter on the top edge.

2 Marking the depth of the molding
Set a marking gauge to the depth required for the molded edge, and scribe a line on the end grain and round to the shoulder line on both sides of the work.

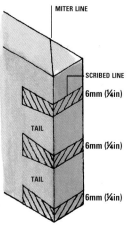

MITER LINE

SCRIBED LINE

6mm (¼in)

TAIL

6mm (¼in)

TAIL

6mm (¼in)

3 Completing the tails
Draw a pencil line 6mm (¼in) below the scribed line, marking the tip of the first tail. Make a similar mark 6mm (¼in) from the other edge. Divide the distance between these lines into the required number of equal-size tails. Saw the waste from between the tails and trim the shoulders square with a chisel. Cut the miter, using a dovetail saw.

4 Marking the pins
Mark the shoulder lines and miter on the pin member as described below left. Chalk the end grain and mark the position of the pins, using the tail member as a template. Square these marks down to the shoulder line on both sides of the workpiece. Use a pencil to mark the waste for the miter and between the pins.

MITER LINE

PIN

PIN

PIN

PIN

5 Cutting the pins and miter
Cut out the waste from between the pins, then reclamp the work in the vise. Holding the dovetail saw at an angle, cut alongside the last pin, down to the line of the miter. Finally, cut the miter itself, then plane or router the molding before assembling the joint.

RABBETED THROUGH DOVETAIL
HAND CUT

It is quite common to cut a rabbet for fitting a tray bottom or to house the back of a cabinet. If you are also planning to incorporate through dovetail joints, it is necessary to extend the shoulder at the bottom edge of each tail member to plug the rabbet at the corner.

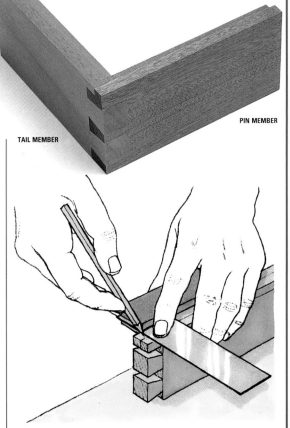

PIN MEMBER

TAIL MEMBER

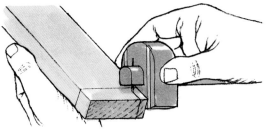

1 Scribing the rabbet depth
Mark the shoulder line for the joint on both sides and across the top edge of the tail member. Set a marking gauge to the depth of the rabbet and scribe a line along the inside of the same workpiece, then across its end and along to the shoulder line on the outside face. Scribe a similar line on the pin member, but only on the inside face.

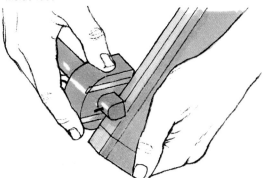

2 Marking the width of the rabbet
Reset the gauge and scribe the width of the rabbet along the bottom edge of both workpieces.

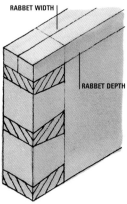

RABBET WIDTH

RABBET DEPTH

3 Marking and cutting the joint
Mark out the required number of equal-size tails, as described opposite, and cut them with a dovetail saw and chisel. Use the tail member as a template for marking out the pins, then cut that half of the joint.

4 Marking the extended shoulder
Mark the extended-shoulder line on the bottom edge of the tail member – the extension should equal the width of the rabbet. Plane a rabbet on each component.

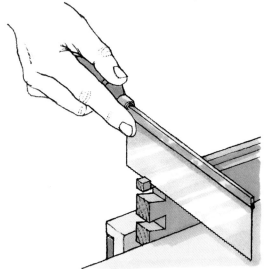

5 Cutting the extended shoulder
Use a dovetail saw to trim the waste back to the extended-shoulder line before assembling the joint.

HALF-BLIND DOVETAIL JOINT
HAND CUT

In traditional drawer construction, it is standard practice to use through dovetails at the back corners while fitting the drawer front, using half-blind dovetail joints that are invisible when the drawer is closed. This is achieved by lapping the pin member over the end of each tail member.

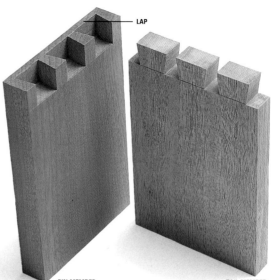

LAP

PIN MEMBER   TAIL MEMBER

1 Marking and cutting the tails
Set a cutting gauge to the thickness of the pin member less the thickness of the lap, which should be at least 3mm (⅛in). Use the gauge to scribe a shoulder line all round the tail member. Set out and cut the tails as described for a through dovetail (see pages 82-3).

2 Marking the pins
Set a cutting gauge to the length of the tails and, working from the inside face of the pin member, scribe the lap line on the end grain. Reset the gauge to the thickness of the tail member and scribe the pin shoulder line across the inside face of the same workpiece. Chalk the end grain and, using the tails as a template, score the shape of the pins in the chalk. From these marks, square parallel lines on the inside face, down to the shoulder line.

3 Cutting the pins
Clamp the work in a bench vise. Holding a dovetail saw at an angle, cut down on the waste side of each line, stopping at the lap and shoulder lines.

4 Sawing out the waste
Before you take the work out of the vise, remove some of the waste from between the pins with the saw.

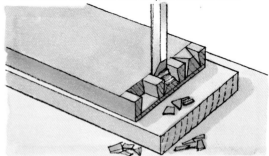

5 Paring down to the lines
Remove what is left of the waste by cutting back to the shoulder line and paring down to the lap line with a bevel-edge chisel. It pays to cut away the wood gradually, making alternate cuts, first across the grain, then parallel with it.

HALF-BLIND DOVETAIL JOINT
MACHINE CUT

A half-blind dovetail joint can be cut with a hand-held power router, using a fixed-finger dovetail jig which enables both the pins and tails to be cut simultaneously. It is a relatively inexpensive jig that produces equal-size, regularly spaced pins and tails. The joint is perfectly functional, but it is necessary to design the width of the components to suit the finger spacing of the jig. Test the jig's settings by cutting test pieces before you proceed with the actual work.

TEMPLATE — TOP CLAMP BAR — EDGE STOP — FRONT CLAMP BAR

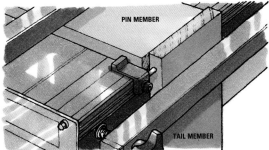

PIN MEMBER / TAIL MEMBER

1 Clamping the work
Mount the tail member vertically in the jig, face-side inwards, then insert the pin member (drawer front) face down, and butt its end grain against the tail member. Slide the pin member up to the jig's edge stop, then offset the tail member sideways by half the finger spacing. Now fit the finger template, which is marked with a 'sight line' that runs centrally down the row of fingers. Adjust it until the sight line corresponds to the butt joint between the two components.

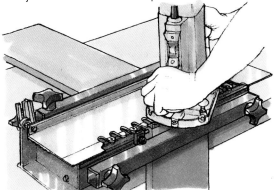

2 Cutting the joint
Prepare the router, fitting the guide bush and dovetail cutter recommended by the jig manufacturer. Working from left to right, feed the cutter between each pair of fingers, keeping the router level and following the template with the guide bush.

3 Assembling the joint
Unclamp the test pieces and rotate one of them through 180 degrees to mate their jointed ends. If the joint fits snugly, cut a similar joint for the other end of the pin member (drawer front), butting it against the edge stop at the other end of the jig.

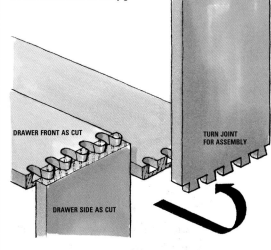

DRAWER FRONT AS CUT / DRAWER SIDE AS CUT / TURN JOINT FOR ASSEMBLY

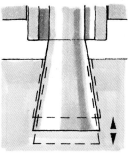

4 Adjusting the cut
If you find the joint is loose, increase the cutting depth of the router slightly. If the joint's too tight, raise the cutter.

5 Modifying sockets
If the sockets are too deep, adjust the finger template forward. If the tail member projects slightly, set the template backwards.

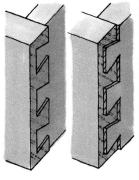

BLIND DOVETAIL JOINT
HAND CUT

Except for a narrow band of end grain, the blind dovetail is virtually undetectable when the joint is assembled. It is used primarily for cabinetmaking or box construction.

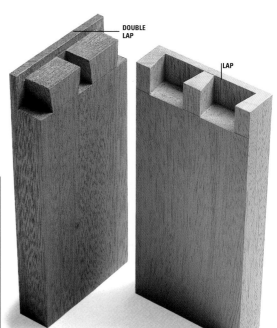

DOUBLE LAP

LAP

TAIL MEMBER   PIN MEMBER

1 Marking the tail member
Set a cutting gauge to the thickness of the pin member and scribe the joint shoulder line on the inside face and edges of the tail member. Reset the gauge to the width of the double lap and, working from the outside face, scribe a line across the end grain and down to the shoulder line on both edges. Use the same setting to scribe the depth of the double lap on the inside face and edges.

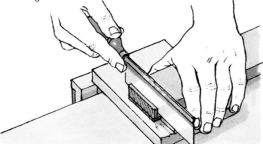

2 Removing the lap waste
Cut the double lap on the end of the tail member, following the gauged lines with a dovetail saw.

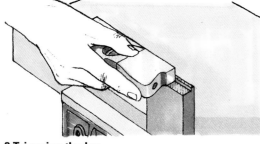

3 Trimming the lap
If necessary, trim the end grain and the inside of the double lap with a shoulder plane, to make sure both surfaces are flat and square.

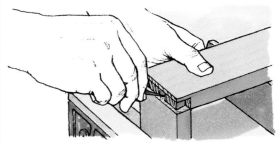

4 Marking and cutting the tails
Mark out the tails with a dovetail template, and square their tips across the end grain. Saw and chisel out the waste as described for cutting the pins in a half-blind dovetail joint (see page 90).

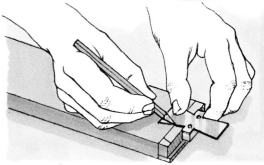

5 Marking and cutting the pins
Scribe the width of the lap on the end of the pin member. Reset the gauge to match the thickness of the tails only and mark the pin shoulder line across the inside face of the workpiece. Chalk the end grain and mark the shape of the pins, using the tails as a template. From these marks, square parallel lines down to the shoulder line on the inside face. Saw and chisel out the waste (see page 90).

MITERED DOVETAIL JOINT
HAND CUT

A mitered dovetail, which is typically used when both components are the same thickness, requires careful marking and cutting. Since it is entirely hidden, it is sometimes referred to as a secret mitered dovetail. Contrary to usual practice, cut the pins first and use them as a template for marking the tails.

MITERS

TAIL MEMBER

PIN MEMBER

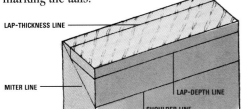

LAP-THICKNESS LINE

MITER LINE

LAP-DEPTH LINE

SHOULDER LINE

1 Marking guide lines
Set a cutting gauge to match the thickness of the wood, and scribe a shoulder line across the inside face of each component. Using a marking knife and miter square, mark the miter on both edges, running from the shoulder line to the outside corner. Reset the gauge to the thickness of the miter lap and, working from the outside face, scribe a line across the end grain. Using the same setting, scribe the depth of the miter lap on the inside face. Cut and trim the lap on each component (see opposite).

4 Bevelling the lap
Trim the lap to a mitered edge with a chisel, working from each end towards the middle. If necessary, finish with a shoulder plane.

2 Marking the pins
Set a marking gauge to 6mm (¼in) and scribe a line parallel with each edge of the work, running up from the shoulder line and across the end grain to the lap. Set out the pins between these lines. A home-made cardboard dovetail template will help space the pins regularly.

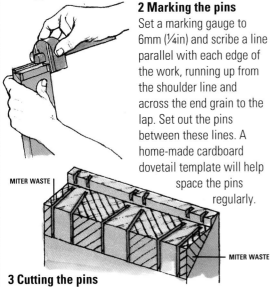

MITER WASTE

MITER WASTE

3 Cutting the pins
From the marks drawn on the end grain, square parallel lines down to the shoulder on the inside face. Saw and chisel out the waste between the pins (see page 90). Don't worry if you saw into the lap. Cut the miter on each edge, following the marked line with a saw.

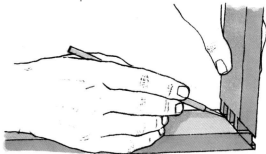

5 Marking and cutting the tails
Lay the tail member flat on a bench. Holding the pin member on end, align its inside face with the shoulder line marked across the tail member. Scribe around the pins to mark the shape of the tails. Square parallel lines across the end grain to mark the tips of the tails. Cut the tails and miters as described for the pins, and miter the lap in the same way.

MOCK DOVETAIL JOINT
MACHINE CUT

The mock dovetail is a mitered butt joint reinforced with tapered splines that create a decorative corner effect similar in appearance to the end-grain pins of a conventional dovetail joint. The first step is to construct the box or carcase with a glued miter joint at each corner (see pages 20–22).

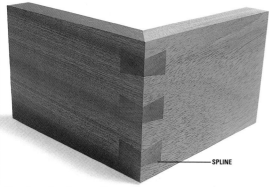

SPLINE

Cutting the dovetails
Set up the fence and jig so that the dovetail cutter fits accurately in the slot in the cradle. Place the workpiece in the cradle, aligning one edge with the marked line, and feed the jig into the cutter to make the first slot. Move the work sideways, slipping the first slot over the locating strip, then make the next cut. Continue in the same way to cut all the dovetail slots.

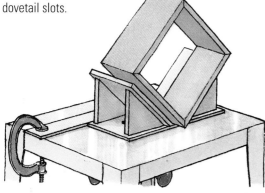

Making dovetail splines
Use the router to machine a strip of wood that fits snugly in the dovetail slots. Cut the strip into short lengths and glue one into each slot. When the glue sets, saw off the waste and plane the spines flush.

MAKING A CRADLE JIG
Construct a cradle from MDF to hold the assembled workpiece at 45 degrees to the router table. Machine a small rectangular opening in the base before you assemble the basic jig with glue. Set the router to cut a dovetail slot in the center of the cradle.

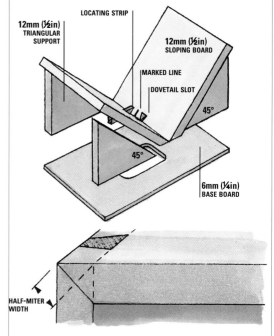

LOCATING STRIP

12mm (½in) TRIANGULAR SUPPORT

12mm (½in) SLOPING BOARD

MARKED LINE

DOVETAIL SLOT

45°

45°

6mm (¼in) BASE BOARD

HALF-MITER WIDTH

1 Cutting the dovetail slot
Measure the width of the miter used to construct the box or carcase, and set the depth of cut on the router to half that width, plus 6mm (¼in) for the jig base. Running the jig along a 6mm (¼in) thick fence clamped to the router table, machine a dovetail slot in the center of the cradle.

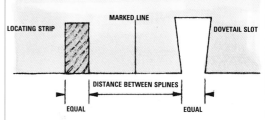

LOCATING STRIP

MARKED LINE

DOVETAIL SLOT

DISTANCE BETWEEN SPLINES

EQUAL

EQUAL

2 Fitting the locating strip
Select a straight cutter that matches the width of the dovetail slot at its base. Machine a straight slot to one side of the dovetail slot, with the distance between them equal to the required spacing of the splines. Glue a tight-fitting strip of wood into it. Mark a line centrally between the dovetail slot and the locating strip.

CHAPTER 11 The finger joint is a product of the machine age – it is perfectly feasible to cut one by hand, but this process is both tedious and time-consuming. A finger joint is a strong and decorative corner joint used for box construction and to make sliding trays and drawers for modern-style furniture.

FINGER JOINTS

FINGER JOINT
MACHINE CUT

Though it cannot compare with the production rate of a commercial spindle molder, it is not too difficult to cut batches of finger joints on a table saw, using a simple jig. Use a blade that will cut a generous kerf between fingers or, for wider spacing, use an adjustable dado blade, where the cutting edge moves from side to side with each revolution. The exact size and spacing of fingers will be determined by the width of your workpiece.

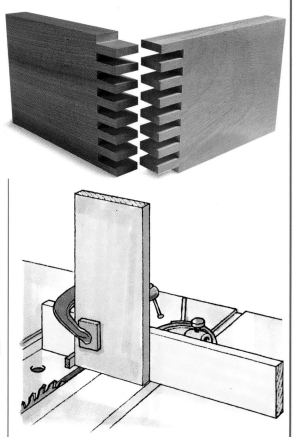

1 Making the jig
Clamp a length of wood or MDF to the saw's sliding miter fence. Adjust the blade height to just over the thickness of the intended workpiece, then make one cut to leave a finger-width slot in the clamped board.

2 Fitting the tongue
Plane a length of hardwood to make a snug fit in the slot. Cut off a short strip and glue it into the slot, forming a tongue that projects about 38mm (1½in) from the face of the board.

3 Positioning the jig
Remove the clamp and slide the jig sideways, sandwiching the offcut from the planed strip between the tongue and saw blade. Clamp or screw the board securely to the fence, and remove the loose strip.

1 Clamping the work
Stand the work on end and butt it against the projecting tongue. Hold it in place with a C-clamp. Although only one workpiece is shown here, you can clamp a number of pieces together and cut them simultaneously.

2 Cutting and locating the work
Feed the work into the blade to cut the first slot, then unclamp the work and fit the slot over the tongue. Replace the clamp and cut the next slot.

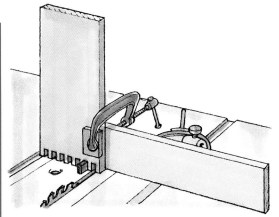

3 Cutting a row of fingers
Continue in the same way until you have completed the row of fingers. To cut a similar joint at the other end of the workpiece, turn it end-for-end, butting the same edge against the tongue, and repeat the sequence.

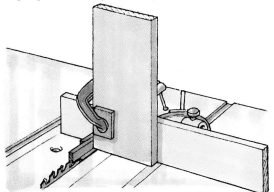

4 Clamping the other half of the joint
The row of fingers in the second component is offset to fit between the fingers you have just cut. Clamp the work as before, but sandwich the offcut strip between it and the tongue.

5 Cutting the second row of fingers
Remove the loose strip and saw a notch in the edge of the work. Remove the clamp, slide the work to locate the notch over the tongue, and clamp it again. Cut a row of fingers as described above, finishing with another notch at the far edge. Flip the work over to cut the other end.

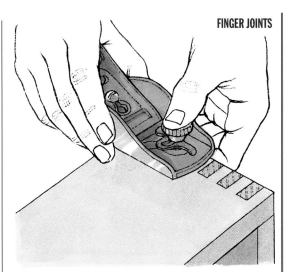

6 Planing the fingers flush
Assemble the joints and, when the glue has set, plane flush the ends of the slightly projecting fingers.

CUTTING FINGER JOINTS ON A RADIAL-ARM SAW
To cut finger joints on a radial-arm saw, rotate the mounting to set the blade in a horizontal plane. To support the work, replace the saw's main guide fence with a small raised table and fence made from MDF.

Clamp four workpieces together on the raised table, with their ends projecting by the required depth of cut. To offset the fingers for one half of each joint, raise two of the components on a packing strip that equals the width of the saw cut.

Begin by adjusting the blade to cut open notches in the raised workpieces, then lower the blade in stages to cut equally spaced fingers on all four components simultaneously.

Raise two components on a packing strip

PACKING STRIP

MOCK FINGER JOINT
MACHINE CUT

At first sight, the mock finger joint looks identical to the genuine article; on closer inspection, however, you notice the fingers are not staggered. It is actually a miter joint with 6mm (¼in) reinforcing splines planed flush. It can be cut with a power router or on a table saw. Whichever method you adopt, first construct the workpiece with glued miter joints.

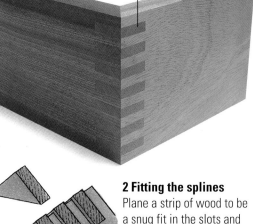

SPLINE

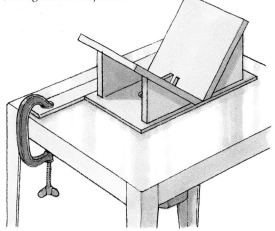

Making a router jig

Make a cradle jig as described for a mock dovetail (see page 94), but rout a straight 6mm (¼in) wide slot in the center of the cradle and another identical slot for the locating strip 6mm (¼in) to one side. Glue a snug-fitting strip of wood into the second slot.

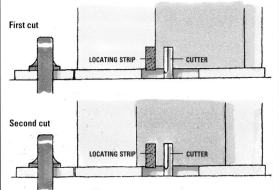

First cut

LOCATING STRIP — CUTTER

Second cut

LOCATING STRIP — CUTTER

1 Slotting the workpiece

Place the assembled workpiece in the cradle, with one edge butted against the locating strip. Feed the work into the router cutter to machine the first slot. Place the slot over the locating strip to reposition the workpiece for cutting the next slot. Continue in a similar way until you have machined the row of slots.

2 Fitting the splines

Plane a strip of wood to be a snug fit in the slots and cut it into 90-degree triangles to make slightly oversize splines. Glue them in place and, when the adhesive has set, plane them flush.

USING A TABLE SAW

Make a simple jig by tilting the saw blade to 45 degrees and ripping a 90-degree V-shape notch down the center of a short length of 50 x 100mm (2 x 4in) softwood. Leave about 6mm (¼in) of wood just below the notch.

Set the blade upright and cut two slots across the base, about one third of the way along the jig. Space the slots to match the required interval between 'fingers', and if you want splines wider than the standard saw kerf, fit an adjustable dado blade. Glue a locating strip in one slot and proceed to cut the joint as described above, using the saw's miter fence to feed the jig.

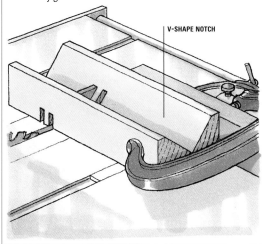

V-SHAPE NOTCH

CHAPTER *12* All but the cheapest drop-leaf tables are made with sophisticated detailing, aimed at making the moving components attractive as well as functional. The joint between leaf and fixed top is invariably molded to hide the actual hinges when the leaf is lowered; on smaller sofa and Pembroke tables, the leaves are supported on brackets fashioned with integral wooden-hinge mechanisms.

KNUCKLE JOINT
HAND CUT

The pivoting wooden brackets that support the lightweight drop leaves of small tables are sometimes fixed to the side rails with metal butt hinges. However, they are traditionally made with stout, integral knuckle joints that are not only stronger but also more sympathetic to a finely made piece. The fixed part of each bracket is screwed to the side rail of the table.

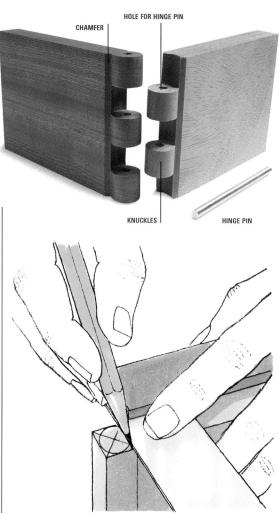

CHAMFER

HOLE FOR HINGE PIN

KNUCKLES

HINGE PIN

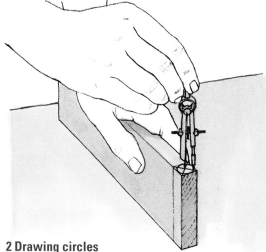

1 Marking out the joints
Set a cutting gauge to the thickness of the wood, and scribe a line all round both halves of the bracket, parallel with the jointed ends. Draw diagonals across the squares formed on each edge of the workpieces.

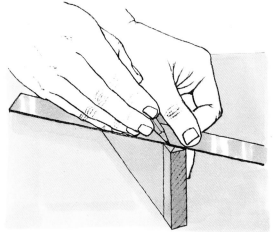

2 Drawing circles
With the point of a compass centered on the intersection of the diagonals, draw a circle in each square, equal to the thickness of the wood.

3 Marking the chamfers
Chamfers are cut along the knuckle shoulders to allow the pivoting half of the bracket to move freely. Mark out the chamfers by drawing lines through the points where each circle bisects the diagonals. Square these lines all round both workpieces.

4 Removing the waste
Saw along each marked chamfer line, down to the circumference of the circle, then chisel out the waste on the knuckle side of the kerf.

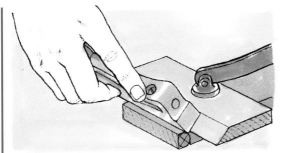

5 Planing the chamfer
Using a 45-degree guide block clamped to the work, accurately cut each chamfer with a shoulder plane.

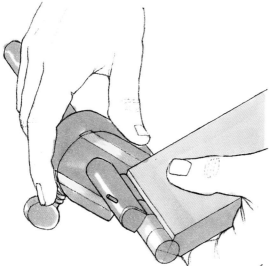

6 Marking the knuckles
Shape the knuckle end of each workpiece with a plane and wood files, then use a marking gauge to divide the rounded sections into five equal parts. Hatch the waste to define three knuckles on one end and two that interlock with them on the other.

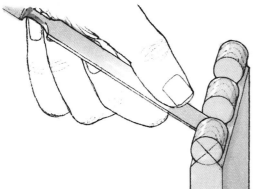

7 Cutting the knuckles
Saw alongside each knuckle down to the chamfer, and remove most of the waste with a coping saw. Working from each side towards the middle, shape the concave shoulder between the knuckles by scooping out the wood with a chisel held bevel-downwards.

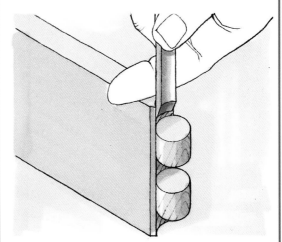

8 Trimming the ends
Shape the open ends of the shoulder with an in-cannel gouge. Try the joint for fit, and relieve any tight spots with a chisel or file.

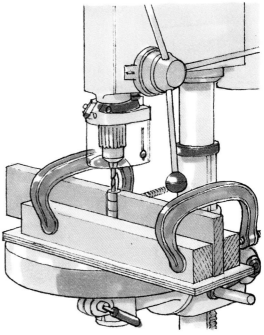

9 Inserting the hinge pin
Assemble the knuckle joint and clamp it between two stout battens to keep both components perfectly aligned. Using a drill press, bore a hole down the center of the knuckles, to take a snug-fitting brass hinge pin. Tap the pin in place and file both ends flush.

RULE JOINT
HAND CUT

This is not a true woodworking joint in the conventional sense, since it does not physically attach one component to another. The rule joint comprises two molded edges, one on a fixed table top and the other on a hinged leaf, that are designed to pivot, one around the other, as the leaf is raised and lowered. Its function is to conceal special back-flap hinges screwed to the undersides of the top and leaf. This type of hinge has flaps of different length, the longer one being screwed to the leaf. Rule-joint moldings are cut before the final shaping of the table top and leaves.

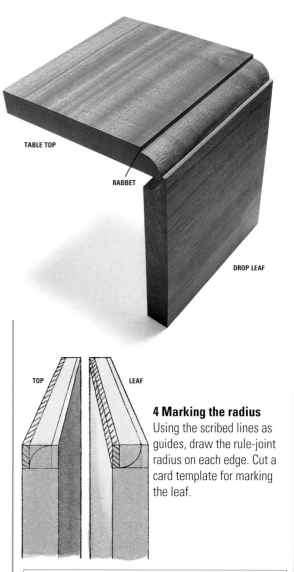

TABLE TOP

RABBET

DROP LEAF

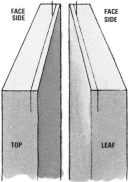

KNUCKLE GAUGE LINES

FACE SIDE

FACE SIDE

TOP

LEAF

1 Gauging the edges
Set a marking gauge to match the radius of the hinge knuckle, and scribe a line along each edge to be molded, working from the undersides of both components. Continue the lines just onto the neighbouring edges.

RABBET LINES

RADIUS DIMENSION

2 Marking the rabbet
Reset the gauge to the depth of the joint rabbet – about 3mm (⅛in) – and scribe similar parallel lines, working from the face side of each workpiece. The distance between the two gauged lines represents the radius of the rule joint.

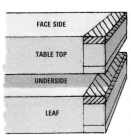

FACE SIDE

TABLE TOP

UNDERSIDE

LEAF

3 Marking the width
With a cutting gauge set to this radius, scribe a line across the face side of the fixed top and across the underside of the leaf. Mark the edges similarly, and hatch the waste.

TOP

LEAF

4 Marking the radius
Using the scribed lines as guides, draw the rule-joint radius on each edge. Cut a card template for marking the leaf.

MAKING A SCRATCH STOCK
To shape the edges of both workpieces, make a scratch stock from hardwood or plywood, and prepare a pair of matched cutters from steel sheet. File the exact radius curve on the convex cutter, but make the concave cutter very slightly smaller.

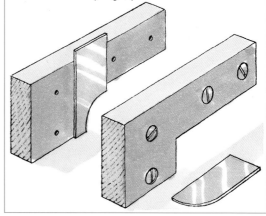

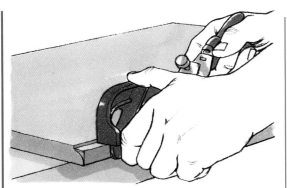

1 Cutting the rabbet
Clamp the table top face-side up on the bench, and cut the joint rabbet down to the marked lines, using a rabbet plane.

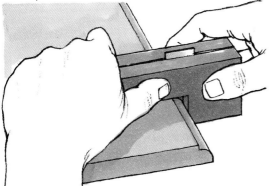

2 Shaping the convex molding
Shape the molding roughly with a plane before finishing with the appropriate cutter clamped in the scratch stock. A sharp cutter should leave a perfectly smooth surface – if necessary, smooth the curve with abrasive paper wrapped round a shaped block.

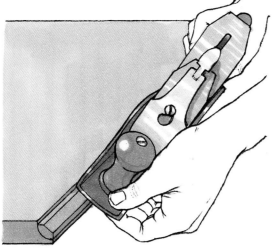

3 Preparing the leaf edge
Clamp the leaf face-side down and cut a rabbet as described above, then plane down the waste as close as possible to the marked radius.

4 Shaping the concave molding
Using a molding plane, remove the waste almost to the marked radius, then finish shaping with the scratch stock. Check both halves of the molding for fit, and reduce any high points with abrasive paper.

5 Marking the hinge recesses
With a cutting gauge set to the rule-joint radius, scribe the center line for each hinge knuckle on the underside of the top, about 150mm (6in) in from the side edges. Lay the leaf and top together, face-down on the bench. Align each hinge with its line and score round it.

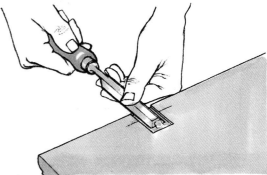

6 Fitting the hinges
Chisel the hinge recesses to set the flaps flush with the surfaces, cutting a slightly deeper recess for each knuckle. Drill a pilot hole for the one screw nearest to the knuckle in each flap, and temporarily screw the hinges in place. Check the movement of the leaf and, if all is well (see page 104), insert the remaining screws.

CORRECTING A MISALIGNED RULE JOINT

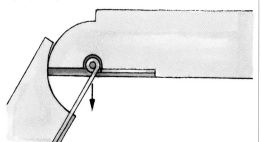

Binding near the rabbet
If the joint binds just before the leaf is level, remove the hinges and pare the hinge recesses until they are slightly deeper.

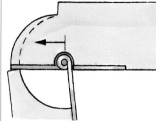

Binding towards the bottom
If the rule joint binds when the leaf is nearly vertical, pack out the hinge flaps with thin card or veneer.

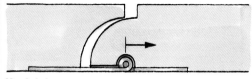

Catching on the lower edge
If the edge of the leaf catches on the underside of the fixed top, the hinges are set too far from the molded edge. Cut the knuckle recesses slightly wider so that you can move the hinges, in order to place the center of each knuckle directly below the rabbet. Plug the old screw holes.

Unsightly gap
If there is an excessive gap between leaf and top when they are level, the hinge knuckles are set too close to the molded edge. Cut the knuckle recesses slightly wider, and extend the flap recesses so that you can reposition both hinges.

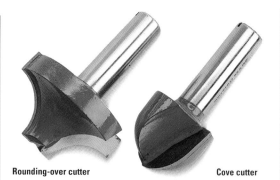

Rounding-over cutter   Cove cutter

Machining a rule joint
A power router is the ideal tool for cutting a rule joint. Matching cutters ensure that the two profiles mate perfectly. Select cutters that will suit the thickness of the table-top panels, and refer to how to establish the radius (see page 102). Typically, 12mm (½in) cutters are used to machine 18mm (¾in) panels. You can cut.both profiles with a hand-held router fitted with self-guiding cutters, but a table-mounted router is preferable.

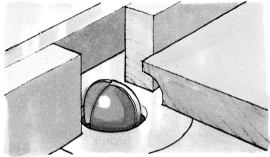

Cutting the concave molding
Fit the cove cutter in the router and then set the guide fence until it is centered accurately on the cutter. Always machine the profile of the molding in stages, raising the cutter between each pass, so that you leave not less than 3mm (⅛in) of wood along the top edge of the workpiece.

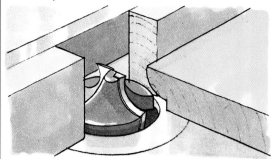

Cutting the convex molding
Swap cutters, and machine the matching profile along the top panel in similar stages. Gradually raise the cutter until the molded edge includes a rabbet that allows the leaf and top to lie flush.

CHAPTER 13 Knock-down joints use a mechanical fitting to hold components together. Manufacturers produce a wide range of ingenious connectors with which you can assemble rigid joints, using little more than a drill and a screwdriver. Chairs, tables, cabinets and bed frames can all be constructed simply from solid wood or man-made boards, utilizing knock-down fittings.

BOLT AND BARREL NUT

This is a strong and positive fitting for all types of frame construction where the end of a rail meets the side of a leg or other vertical member. The bolt passes through a counterbored hole in the leg and into the end of the rail, where it is then screwed into a threaded barrel nut located in a stopped hole. A screw slot in the end of the nut allows you to align the threaded hole with the bolt. A wooden locating dowel fitted in the end of the rail makes assembly easier and prevents the rail from turning as the bolt is tightened.

3 Fitting the locating dowel

Tap a brad into the end of the rail on its center line, about 12mm (½in) from one edge. Crop the head off the brad, then assemble and tighten the fitting. Dismantle the joint, and drill a 6mm (¼in) stopped hole in the leg where the cropped brad left a mark. Remove the brad and drill the rail in the same way as the leg, then glue a short dowel in the hole.

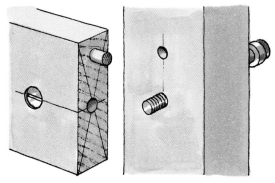

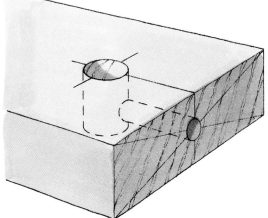

1 Drilling the rail

Draw diagonals across the end of the rail to find the center, and bore a clearance hole for the bolt where the lines cross. Calculate the distance from the end of the rail for the barrel nut, and drill a stopped hole in the side of the rail to intercept the bolt hole.

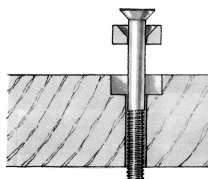

2 Drilling the leg

Mark and drill a counterbored clearance hole for the bolt and collar in the leg.

TEE NUTS AND BOLTS

A tee nut is an internally threaded collar with an integral spiked washer that provides a firm anchor for a bolt fixing. A relatively crude fitting, it is probably best reserved for upholstered frames.

Fitting a tee nut

Clamp the components together and drill an 8mm (5⁄16in) clearance hole through both parts. Tap the nut into the back of one component and pass the bolt through the other. Tighten the bolt to pull the parts together, and seat the nut securely in the wood.

CORNER PLATES

Pressed-metal corner plates form demountable
joints between table legs and rails. The flanges are
located in shallow slots cut across the inside of
each rail, and the plate is held in place by woodscrews. A threaded hanger bolt, screwed into a
chamfer planed on the inner corner of the leg, is
fixed to the plate with a wing nut. Tightening the
nut pulls the leg hard up against the square-cut
shoulders of the rails.

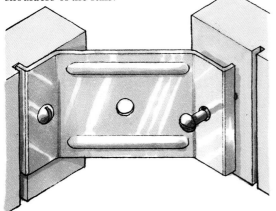

1 Preparing the rails
Cut the rails to length. Calculate the flange-slot
positions from the size of the legs and plates, and draw
squared guide lines across the rails. Cut the slots to the
required depth, and screw the plates to the rails.

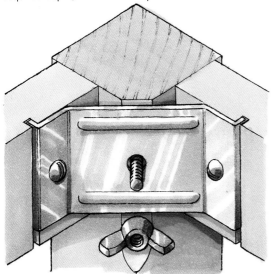

2 Preparing the legs
Cut the legs to length, and plane or chisel a stopped
chamfer on the inside of each one. Screw a hanger bolt
into the leg (see top right) so that it mates with the
plate-fixing hole. Clamp each leg with a wing nut.

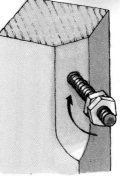

Inserting hanger bolts
Fit two hexagonal nuts on a
bolt and lock them together
by turning them in opposite
directions with a pair of
spanners. Drive the bolt
into a pilot hole drilled in
the leg, using one spanner
located on the nuts. When
the bolt is fully in place,
remove the nuts.

CABINET CONNECTORS
*Cabinet connectors bolt together adjoining cupboards
and help keep them aligned. The bolt passes through
a hole in one side panel into the ribbed 'nut', which
fits tightly in a hole drilled in the neighbouring panel.
The fitting is removable.*

Fitting the connectors
Mount the cabinets side-
by-side and drill two 8mm
(⁵⁄₁₆in) holes through both
adjoining side panels,
one near the base of the
cupboard and the other
near the top. Insert the
connectors and tighten
both bolts.

CHIPBOARD FASTENERS

You can improve the strength of screwed joints in chipboard by fitting nylon inserts into the square-cut edges. These chipboard fasteners plug into pre-drilled holes and expand to grip the material as the screw is tightened.

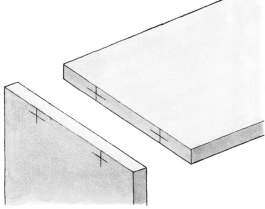

1 Marking the panels
Cut the boards square and, using a marking gauge, scribe a center line on the end of one component. Depending on the width of the boards, mark off two or more screw centers. Mark matching centers on the face of the other component.

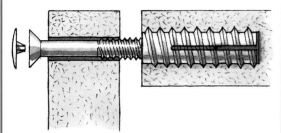

2 Making the joint
Bore screw-shank clearance holes through the side panel, and larger stopped holes for the nylon fasteners in the edge of the other component. Countersink the clearance holes, if necessary, then insert the fasteners and assemble the joint.

SCREW CONNECTORS

These bright-galvanized or black-finished screw fittings have coarse threads that make secure butt joints without inserts. The shallow, countersunk heads are cross-slotted or have a hexagonal socket that is driven with a cranked key.

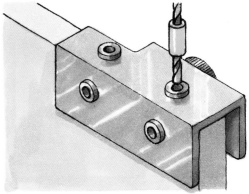

1 Drilling stopped holes in the edge
A special jig holds the drill bit perpendicular to the surface. Mount the jig on the end of the horizontal component and align it with screw centers marked across the workpiece. Clamp the jig, and drill stopped holes for the threaded screw shanks.

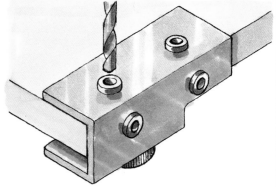

2 Drilling clearance holes
Clamp the jig over the end of the upright component, aligning it with similar screw centers. Bore clearance holes through the panel, using the boss on the side of the jig to guide the drill bit. Screw the joint together — only hard plastic-faced materials need countersinking.

SCREW SOCKETS

Threaded-metal screw sockets provide secure fixing points for bolting together wood frames or man-made boards. A coarse thread on the outside of each fitting pulls the socket into a stopped hole drilled in the face of one component. A finer thread on the inside of the fitting receives a metal bolt that holds the other component in place.

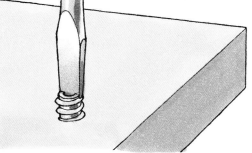

1 Fitting a socket
Bore an 8mm (5⁄16in) diameter stopped hole deep enough to set the socket just below the surface of the workpiece. Drive the fitting into the hole, using a screwdriver in the slot cut across the end of the socket.

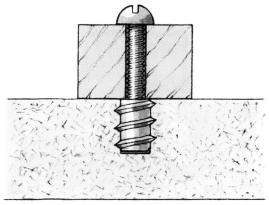

2 Assembling the components
Mark the center of a clearance hole for the bolt in the other component and drill right through it, taking care not to splinter the wood fibers on the underside. Assemble the two halves of the joint, clamping them tightly with the bolt.

BLOCK JOINTS

This inexpensive, surface-mounted fitting consists of interlocking plastic blocks screwed on the inside of cabinet corners. Molded dowels on one half of the joint locate with sockets in the other. When two panels have been joined at right angles, the block fittings are clamped together with a bolt.

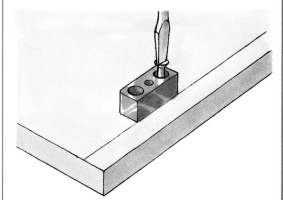

1 Fitting the socket blocks
Mark the thickness of the board on the inside of the carcase side panel. Mark the positions of two block joints about 50mm (2in) from the front and back edges. Align the base of each socket block with the marked lines, and screw it to the panel.

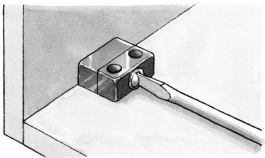

2 Fitting the dowel blocks
Holding the panels together at right angles, fit the mating dowel blocks and mark their fixing holes on the other board. Screw the blocks in place, and assemble the joint with the clamping bolts.

CAM FITTINGS

The cam fitting is a discreet knock-down joint for carcases constructed from man-made boards. It is used to make corner joints, or for holding shelves and vertical dividers. A round-head metal dowel screwed into the vertical component or side panel locates with a cam-action boss set in the underside of the horizontal component or shelf. Turning the boss with a screwdriver pulls the joint tight. The standard straight dowel is made with a coarse thread that screws directly into the board. Another type of dowel screws into a plastic or metal insert. Double-ended dowels secure straight end-to-end joints, and a cranked version is used for miters.

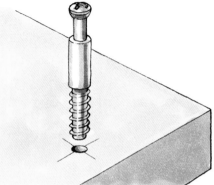

1 Fitting the dowels

For a corner joint, set a marking gauge to half the thickness of the board and scribe a line on the inside of the side panel. Mark off two centers equidistant from each edge; a wide panel may require another dowel in the middle. Drill pilot holes for coarse-threaded dowels, and screw them in place.

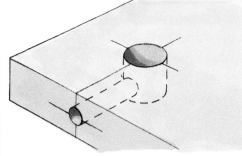

2 Inserting cam-action bosses

Scribe a line centrally on the end of the shelf and, using the side panel as a guide, mark out the positions of clearance holes for the dowels. Drill the holes to the required depth. On the underside, use a Forstner bit to drill stopped holes that intercept the center of the dowel holes, and insert the bosses.

3 Assembling the joint

Each boss is marked with an arrow that should point towards the side panel. Assemble the joint with a dowel in each hole, then turn the bosses with a screwdriver to lock the components together.

CHAPTER *14* Although woodworking machinery produces work with ease and accuracy, handtools are still important in joint-making. It is often more convenient to hand-make a limited number of joints, and it is impossible to make certain joints with a power tool. This glossary lists joint-making hand-tools, power tools and machinery; special jigs and templates are found with the relevant joints.

TOOLS & MACHINES

MEASURING AND MARKING TOOLS

Accurate marking-out is the key to good joint-making. A few basic tools enable you to measure out workpieces and to scribe dimension lines on solid wood and man-made boards.

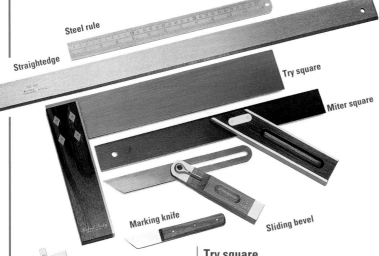

Steel rule
Straightedge
Try square
Miter square
Marking knife
Sliding bevel
Dovetail template
Retractable tape

Steel rule
A metalworker's steel rule is useful for taking precise measurements, and doubles as a short straightedge for scribing dimension lines on a workpiece with a marking knife.

Straightedge
A strip of steel with one bevelled edge is useful for marking out long, straight lines, and is essential for checking that a surface is cut or planed flat.

Retractable tape measure
A good-quality, flexible steel tape measure is ideal for measuring all but the smallest workpieces. Choose one that is about 5m (16ft) long and is calibrated for both imperial and metric dimensions, so that you can convert one system to the other quickly and easily .

Try square
A necessary tool for checking the accuracy of right-angle joints and for marking lines at 90 degrees to an edge. Choose a square with a 300mm (1ft) blade.

Miter square
The blade of a miter square passes through the stock at an angle of 45 degrees. It is used to mark out and check the accuracy of miter joints.

Sliding bevel
A sliding bevel is used for the same purpose as a miter square, but its blade is adjustable to any angle.

Marking knife
The blade of a woodworker's marking knife is ground to a bevel on one side only, so that its flat face can be run against a steel rule or the blade of a square.

Dovetail template
A template designed for marking out standard dovetails. One blade is made for tails with a slope of 1:6, for softwoods, and the other slopes at 1:8, for hardwoods.

Marking gauge
Use a marking gauge to scribe a line parallel to a planed edge. It is made with a sharp steel pin fixed at one end of a wooden beam. A fence or 'stock' that slides along the beam is clamped at the required distance from the pin, using a brass or plastic thumbscrew. The stock on a good-quality gauge is made with inset brass strips, to prevent wear.

Cutting gauge
Similar to a marking gauge, this tool is fitted with a small blade that passes through the beam and is held in place by a shallow metal wedge. It is used for marking lines across grain, where the pin of a marking gauge would tear the wood fibers.

Mortise gauge
A marking gauge with a second, adjustable pin, used for scoring the two parallel sides of a mortise or tenon simultaneously. Most mortise gauges have another single pin on the opposite side of the beam, so that the tool can also be used as a standard marking gauge.

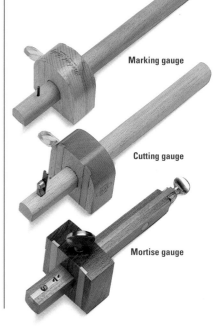

Marking gauge

Cutting gauge

Mortise gauge

HANDSAWS

Backsaws, with their stiffened blades and relatively fine teeth, are ideal for precise joint-making. Frame saws, designed for cutting curves, are useful tools for removing waste from intricate joints.

Tenon saw (traditional pattern)

Tenon saw

The general-purpose tenon saw is perfect for cutting most workpieces square and for sawing comparatively large joints. A well-balanced tenon saw with a 250 to 300mm (10 to 12in) blade is comfortable to use for extended periods.

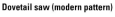

Dovetail saw (traditional pattern)

Dovetail saw

A dovetail saw has even smaller teeth than the tenon saw, and is reserved for cutting fine joints in hardwoods. You can get a 200mm (8in) dovetail saw with either a traditional-pattern closed grip or a straight handle and a longer blade.

Dovetail saw (modern pattern)

Coping saw

A lightweight frame saw with a 150mm (6in) blade held under tension, the coping saw is useful for removing the waste from between dovetails and similar joints. The very narrow blades are replaced when blunt or broken.

Coping saw

PLANES

Bench planes are general-purpose tools used to smooth the surfaces of timber and to plane it square and true. Wooden planes are still available, but nearly all planes are now made from metal. In addition, you will need a few specialized planes for shaping and trimming joints.

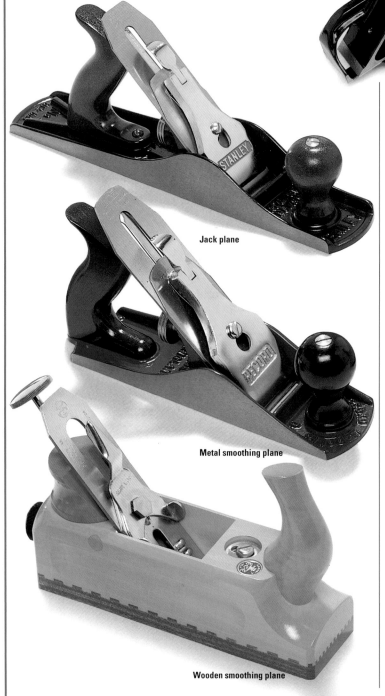

Jack plane

Metal smoothing plane

Wooden smoothing plane

Rabbet plane
This is no longer an essential tool, now that power routers are widespread, but rabbeting is surprisingly fast by hand. The plane has an adjustable fence and depth stop; with the blade mounted near the toe, you can cut stopped rabbets. The pointed spur mounted on the side of the plane scores the wood ahead of the blade when rabbeting across the grain.

Jack plane
The 350mm (1ft 2in) jack plane is long enough to plane most edges accurately. An even longer version, the try plane, is perfect for preparing edge-to-edge butt joints, but is expensive, so most woodworkers manage with the jack plane.

Smoothing plane
The smoothing plane is the smallest bench plane available, at 225mm (9in) long, and is ideal for final shaping and finishing of workpieces. Some woodworkers prefer the feel of a wooden smoothing plane, with its distinctive ergonomic grip and lignum-vitae sole.

Shoulder plane (top)

A dedicated joint-cutting tool, the all-metal shoulder plane is designed specifically for shaving square shoulders on larger joints. Its blade is set at a low angle to enable it to slice through end grain.

Bull-nose plane (above)

A miniature version of the shoulder plane, the bull-nose plane is useful for trimming small joints.

Block plane

A block plane is small enough to be used single-handedly, yet strong enough to take generous shavings for fast shaping and trimming. It is a good general-purpose plane, much used for cutting end grain.

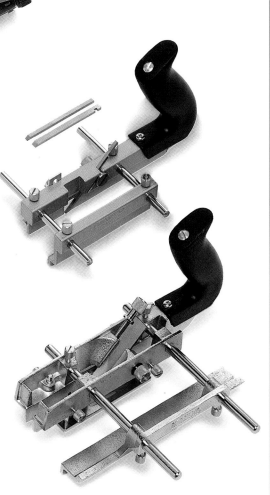

Plow plane (top)

An inexpensive plane, used for cutting narrow grooves parallel with an edge, this comes with a range of interchangeable cutters, from 3 to 12mm (⅛ to ½in) wide. Plow planes are fitted with a strong side fence and a depth stop.

Combination plane (above)

The sophisticated combination plane cuts even wider grooves than a plow plane, and can be used to shape a matching tongue along the edge of another component. The tool can also be modified to plane a raised bead along a tongued edge.

Router plane (left)

Once the preferred tool for levelling dados and hinge recesses, the hand router plane has largely been superseded by the power router. Nevertheless, because of its relative cheapness and simplicity, it is still a worthy tool, and is capable of very accurate work. Special adjustable cutters are made for levelling square and dovetail dados.

CHISELS AND GOUGES

Woodworking of any kind is impossible without at least a small range of well-made chisels and gouges. In joint-making, they are especially useful for removing waste wood and for paring components to make a snug fit.

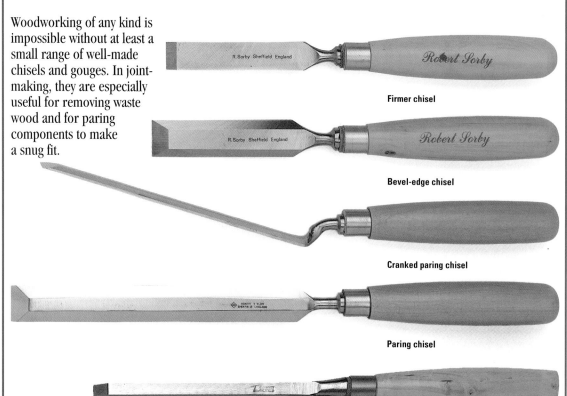

Firmer chisel

Bevel-edge chisel

Cranked paring chisel

Paring chisel

Sash-mortise chisel

Firmer chisel
The standard woodworking chisel has a strong rectangular-section blade which you can confidently drive with a mallet through pine or hardwoods, without fear of it breaking. Firmer chisels range from 3 to 38mm (⅛ to 1½in) wide.

Bevel-edge chisel
The slim-bladed bevel-edge chisel is designed for more delicate work, using hand pressure only. It is used primarily for shaping and trimming joints, and the bevels ground along both sides of the blade make the chisel suitable for working dovetail undercuts. Bevel-edge chisels are made to the same widths as firmers.

Paring chisel
A paring chisel is a bevel-edge chisel with an extra-long blade for levelling dados. A cranked version makes it possible to pare waste from very wide joints.

Sash-mortise chisel
This is a specialized chisel for cutting deep mortises. It is made with a tapered blade that does not jam in the work, and which is thick enough to be used as a lever when chopping waste out of a joint. The deep blade sides help keep it square to the mortise. Mortise chisels are made up to 12mm (½in) wide.

Firmer gouges
A gouge is a chisel with a blade curved in cross section. When the cutting-edge bevel is ground on the inside of the blade, it is known as an in-cannel gouge; the tip of an out-cannel blade is ground on the outside. Gouges are used to scoop waste wood out of hollows and to trim curved shoulders. They average from 6 to 25mm (¼ to 1in) wide.

In-cannel gouge   **Out-cannel gouge**

HAMMERS AND MALLETS

Most workshops boast a range of hammers, even though they are rarely used in joint-making, except when reinforcing with brads or nails.

Cross-peen hammer

Cross-peen hammer (square pattern)

Pin hammer

Pin hammer (square pattern)

Claw hammer

Cross-peen hammer
One medium-weight cross-peen hammer will suffice for most needs. It is heavy enough to tap joints together and dismantle them again, yet sufficiently well-balanced so that you can perform precise operations, such as starting a nail or brad with the wedge-shape peen on the back of the hammer head.

Pin hammer
For delicate work, such as nailing small picture-frame miters, use a lightweight cross-peen pin hammer.

Claw hammer
You will find a claw hammer convenient for making jigs and mock-ups from softwood. Not only can you drive in large nails with ease, but you can also extract them with the split peen, using the strong shaft as a lever. Though slightly more expensive, all-metal claw hammers are even stronger than those with wooden shafts.

Nail set
A nail set is a tapered metal punch that is used with a hammer to drive nail heads below a wood surface.

Carpenter's mallet
Although you can drive plastic-handle chisels and gouges with a metal hammer, you will need to use a mallet for those with wooden handles, to prevent them splitting. This tool is specially designed for the job; its wide head is tapered so that it will strike a chisel squarely each time, and will wedge itself even more securely on the tapered shaft with each blow.

SCREWDRIVERS

Nowadays, many woodworkers use a power screwdriver or at least a large pump-action driver for any form of batch production involving a number of screw fixings. However, in reality you need no more than a handful of basic screwdrivers for driving simple straight-slot and cross-head screws.

Cabinet screwdriver

The standard, general-purpose woodworking screwdriver has a relatively large, oval-shape plastic or wooden grip that fits comfortably in the palm of the hand. The traditional flat tip may be ground from a cylindrical shaft or flared and then ground back to a tapered tip. The tip must fit the screw slot snugly, so it is worth investing in a range of screwdriver sizes.

Cross-head screwdriver

Traditional-pattern woodscrews and modern, fast-action, double-helical screws are both made with cross-shape slots to improve the grip between the screwdriver tip and screw. The matching screwdrivers are made with pointed tips ground with four flutes.

Screwdriver bits

Straight-slot and cross-head bits are available for use with power screwdrivers or variable-speed electric drills.

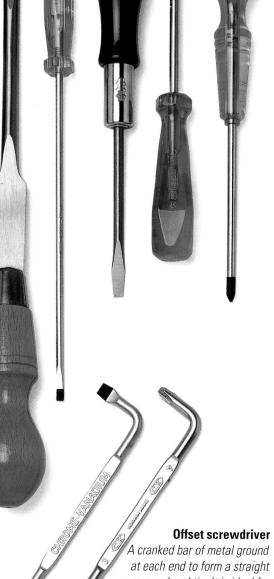

From left to right
Modern cabinet screwdriver
Traditional cabinet screwdriver
Fluted-handled screwdriver
Ratchet screwdriver
Posidriv screwdriver
Phillips screwdriver

Offset screwdriver
A cranked bar of metal ground at each end to form a straight or cross-head tip. It is ideal for inserting knock-down joints that would be inaccessible using a conventional screwdriver.

POWER DRILLS

The power drill is one of the few examples where one can be categorical in saying that a power tool has definite advantages over a handtool in every respect. You can bore large and small holes quickly, cleanly and accurately (in metal as well as wood), and if you opt for a battery-powered (cordless) drill, you can also work away from a mains supply.

Chuck key

Drill-and-countersink bit

CHUCK

Chuck capacity
Most drill chucks incorporate three self-centering jaws that grip the drill bit, and which are operated by a key supplied with the drill. Some drills are fitted with fast-action chucks that open and close the jaws by simply pulling back and releasing the chuck collar. Although it is not essential for most jointing operations, it pays to choose a drill with the largest chuck capacity possible, so that you can fit any of the drill bits and accessories available. Most drills have a chuck capacity of 10 or 13mm (⅜ or ½in).

Speed selection
All but the most basic power drills have variable-speed trigger control – the speed increases as you apply more pressure to the trigger. It is usually possible to pre-select the maximum speed. High speeds are best for boring holes cleanly in wood, but you will need a slower speed for drilling metal and masonry, and for using special bits to drive woodscrews.

Trigger lock
Depressing a small button locks the trigger for continuous running when the drill is mounted in a drill stand (see page 34).

REVERSE-ACTION SWITCH

SPEED SELECTOR

TRIGGER LOCK

Reverse action
Reversing the direction of rotation allows you to remove screws.

Dowel bit
A dowel bit is a woodworking twist drill with a sharp central point that holds the bit on line, and a 'spur' on each side that severs the wood fibers cleanly, making a neat hole.

Drill-and-countersink bit
This special bit drills a pilot hole, shank-clearance hole and counter-sink for a woodscrew in one operation. The only disadvantage is that you need a different bit for each size of screw.

Forstner bit
This drill bit bores clean, flat-bottom holes, ideal for inserting cam fittings (see page 110) and modern kitchen-cabinet hinges.

BOSCH

CSB 500 RE

500W · Beton ⌀ max 15 mm · electronic

Dowel bit   Forstner bit

BISCUIT JOINTER

Biscuit jointers cut narrow slots for small oval plates, or biscuits, of compressed wood that act like dowels for reinforcing butt joints. Biscuits are manufactured in three sizes, to suit different thicknesses of board. You will need to cut the basic joint first, using handtools or other power tools.

Depth of cut
Jointers are fitted with a miniature circular-saw blade that can cut 4mm (5⁄32in) slots up to 22mm (7⁄8in) deep. An adjustable depth stop prevents the tool from plunging too deeply.

Plunge action
Depending on the model, pressing down or pivoting the body of the tool 'plunges' the rotating blade into the work. A spring lifts the blade out again when pressure is released.

DEPTH STOP

GUIDE FENCE

Biscuits

Wood-trimming blade

Jointing blade

Guide fence
An adjustable fence positions the slots accurately in relation to the edge of the work.

POWER ROUTERS

One of the most versatile woodworking tools, the power router will cut grooves, dados and rabbets with ease, and operates at such high speeds that it molds the edges of workpieces quickly and cleanly. With this potential for accuracy, making joints with a router is a pleasure – even cutting complicated dovetails is effortless, and snug-fitting joints are virtually guaranteed.

Plunge mechanism
Most routers are designed on similar lines, with a cutter mounted directly below a motor housing supported on spring-loaded columns above a roughly circular base. Downward pressure on the control handles feeds the cutter through the base and into the wood. The plunge mechanism is locked in that configuration until the particular routing operation is complete. When the lock is released, the springs automatically lift the cutter clear of the work.

Collet capacity
The shank of a cutter fits in a tapered collet in the base of the motor housing, where it is secured with a locknut. Collet sizes of 6 and 8mm (¼ and ⅜in) are common, though you can get routers with 12mm (½in) collets. In any case, collet capacity is not necessarily a limiting factor on cutter size, as most cutters are made with small-size shanks.

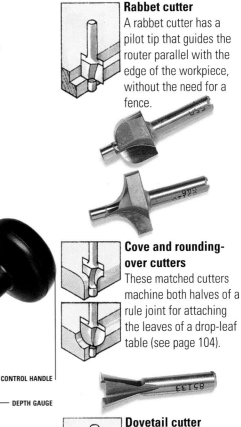

MOTOR HOUSING

BOSCH POF 52 500 W · 27000/min

CONTROL HANDLE

COLLET NUT

CUTTER

PLUNGE MECHANISM

CONTROL HANDLE

DEPTH GAUGE

BASE

ROUTER CUTTERS
Good-quality router cutters are made in a great range of profiles. However, only a limited selection is required for joint-making.

Straight cutter
A straight cutter is used to machine grooves and dados. It is worth buying double-fluted cutters for a better-than-average finish.

Rabbet cutter
A rabbet cutter has a pilot tip that guides the router parallel with the edge of the workpiece, without the need for a fence.

Cove and rounding-over cutters
These matched cutters machine both halves of a rule joint for attaching the leaves of a drop-leaf table (see page 104).

Dovetail cutter
This produces dovetail joints with the aid of proprietary jigs (see pages 84 and 91).

TABLE SAWS

A table saw may not appear to be an obvious choice for cutting woodworking joints, as it is primarily designed for converting timber and man-made boards. However, with its sturdy fences and guides, it is capable of very precise work.

MITER FENCE

RIP FENCE

BLADE-ANGLE CONTROL

BLADE-HEIGHT CONTROL

STARTRITE tilt arbor

Dado head

Saw blades

Since no-one buys a table saw merely to cut joints, it pays to choose a machine with a blade that can cope with more demanding work. A 300mm (1ft) diameter blade is ideal, but you can get by with a 250mm (10in) blade. Special-purpose blades are available for ripping or cross-cutting, but a general-purpose blade with carbide-tipped teeth will prove to be more useful in an amateur workshop. A table-saw blade can be raised or lowered to affect the depth of cut. It can also be cranked to any angle from vertical to 45 degrees, for cutting miters.

Rip fence

Make sure the saw you choose is fitted with a well-mounted adjustable fence to guide the work on straight cuts into the blade. If the free end of the fence is able to flex, the saw is unsuitable for serious woodwork. Also, make sure the rip fence can be adjusted smoothly by very small increments.

Miter fence

Even more important for cutting

joints is a sliding miter fence, for cross-cutting a workpiece from 90 to 45 degrees. Ensure that the fence is sturdy and operates smoothly, and check that it can be fitted with an extended face for handling long workpieces (see page 21).

Dado head

A dado head – a pair of circular-saw blades with 'chipper' blades sandwiched between them – will cut wide dados in one pass. Alternatively, use an adjustable dado blade that cants at an angle, so that the cutting edge moves from side to side with each revolution.

RADIAL-ARM SAWS

The versatility of a well-made radial-arm saw makes it a popular choice for the home workshop. It is ideal for square and mitered crosscuts and, with modification, can be used to cut rabbets, grooves and dados.

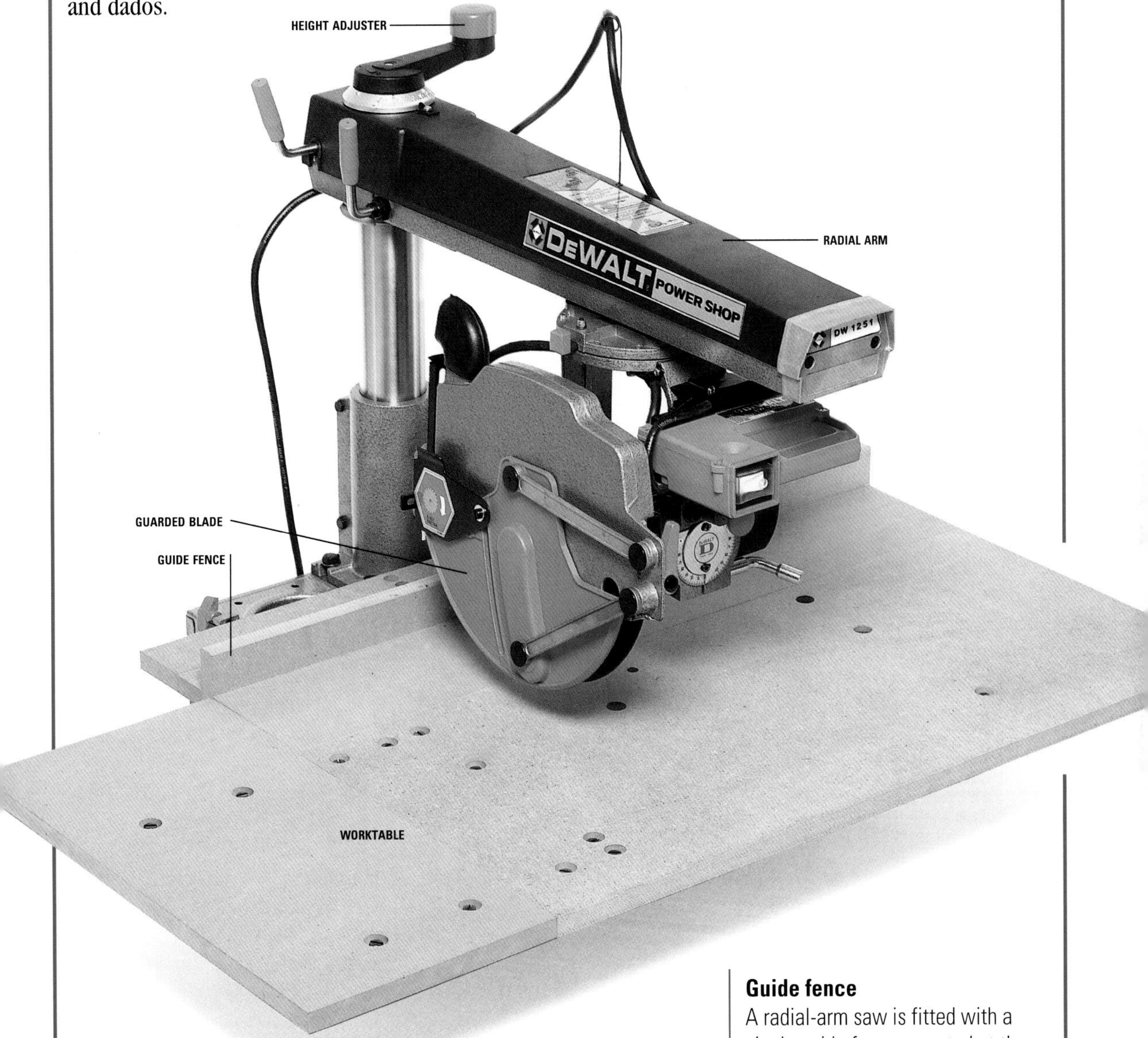

HEIGHT ADJUSTER

RADIAL ARM

GUARDED BLADE

GUIDE FENCE

WORKTABLE

Saw blades

Radial-arm-saw blades are similar to those used for a table saw but, except for industrial machines, they are generally fitted with 250mm (10in) blades only. The depth of cut is altered by adjusting the height of the saw's projecting arm, which raises and lowers the entire saw-blade assembly. The arm can be swung sideways to make angled cuts in the horizontal plane, and tilting the saw-blade assembly enables you to cut miters from 45 to 90 degrees vertically. This feature makes cutting compound miters a very simple task.

Guide fence

A radial-arm saw is fitted with a single guide fence mounted at the back of the worktable. When making crosscuts, the work is held firmly against the fence and the blade assembly pulled towards the operator. When ripping timber and boards, the blade is pivoted parallel to the fence and bolted in place before the work is fed forward against the fence.

WOODWORKING CLAMPS

Interlocking woodworking joints are designed to ensure optimum contact area between components, so that they bond well with adhesive. A well-cut joint requires the minimum of clamping pressure, the main purpose of using clamps being to help assemble the workpiece and hold the parts together while the glue sets. It is always useful to have plenty of clamps available, but pairs of each type in a couple of sizes should suffice. Complete sets of clamps are relatively expensive, but you can acquire them over a period of time or hire them as required.

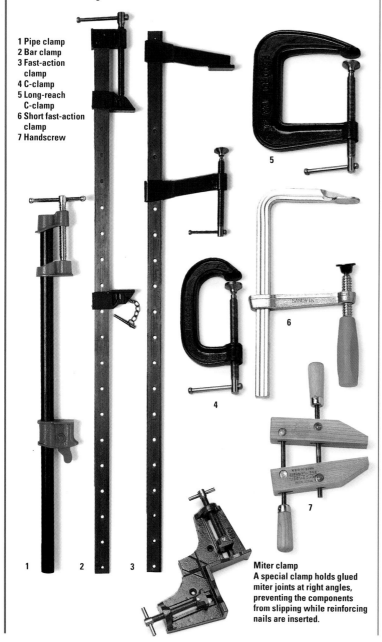

1 Pipe clamp
2 Bar clamp
3 Fast-action clamp
4 C-clamp
5 Long-reach C-clamp
6 Short fast-action clamp
7 Handscrew

Miter clamp
A special clamp holds glued miter joints at right angles, preventing the components from slipping while reinforcing nails are inserted.

Fast-action clamps
Fast-action clamps are designed for speedy adjustment to fit the size of the work. Various versions are available. The bar type has two movable jaws, one of which is also screw-adjustable. On the smaller version of the clamp, only the screw-adjustable jaw is movable. A lightweight clamp has wooden jaws with a cam-action that provides clamping force.

Handscrews
A traditional clamp with wide wooden jaws that can be set to apply even pressure over a broad area. A handscrew is particularly useful when assembling out-of-square frames or for clamping tapered workpieces.

Bar clamps
Bar clamps are used for assembling large frames, panels and carcasses. A bar clamp has a screw-adjustable jaw attached to one end of a flat steel bar. To accommodate assemblies of different sizes, a second movable jaw slides along the bar and is secured at the required position with a tapered steel pin, that passes behind the jaw into one of a series of holes in the bar. The clamps range from 450 to 1200mm (1ft 6in to 4ft) in length.

C-clamps
The C-clamp is an excellent general-purpose clamp that is often used to hold wood to a bench while you work on it. Usually made from cast iron, the frame forms a fixed jaw. Clamping force is applied by a screw, fitted with a ball-jointed shoe. C-clamps are manufactured in many sizes.

Pipe clamps
Similar in most respects to bar clamps, the jaws are attached to a length of round steel pipe.

SETTING UP FOR CLAMPING

When gluing up any assembly, it pays to prepare the work area and rehearse the procedure in advance. This avoids delays that could lead to complications, especially when using a fast-setting adhesive. Assemble the parts without glue, to work out how many clamps you need and to allow you to adjust them to fit the work. You will find a helper most useful when clamping large or complicated assemblies.

It isn't necessary to glue every joint at once. For example, glue the legs and end rails of a table frame first; when these are set, glue the side rails between them. (See page 26 for clamping a solid-wood panel, using edge-to-edge butt joints.)

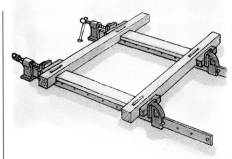

Block aligned

Block misaligned

CLAMPING A FRAME

The majority of frame and carcass joints need clamping in order to hold the assembly square until the adhesive sets. Prepare a pair of bar or pipe clamps, adjusting them so that the assembled frame fits between the jaws, allowing for softwood blocks to protect the work from the metal clamp heads. Carefully position the blocks to align with each joint – a misplaced or undersize block can distort the joint and bruise the wood.

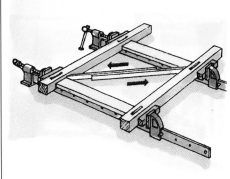

1 Aligning the clamps

MAKING RUBBED JOINTS

Small, accurately cut edge-to-edge joints can be assembled without clamps. Apply glue to both parts and rub them together, squeezing out air and adhesive until atmospheric pressure holds the surfaces in contact while the glue sets.

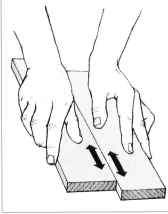

2 Making pinch rods

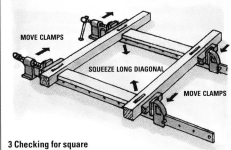

MOVE CLAMPS

SQUEEZE LONG DIAGONAL

MOVE CLAMPS

3 Checking for square

1 Aligning the clamps
Apply adhesive evenly to both parts of each joint. Assemble the frame, ensuring that the clamps are perfectly aligned with their respective rails, and gradually tighten the jaws to close the joints. Wipe off excess adhesive squeezed from the joints, using a damp cloth.

2 Making pinch rods
You can check the accuracy of a small frame with a try square at each corner, but for larger ones, measure the diagonals to ensure they are identical. Make a pair of pinch rods from thin strips of wood, planing a bevel on one end of each rod. Holding the rods back to back, slide them sideways until they fit diagonally across the frame, with a bevelled end tucked into each corner.

3 Checking for square
Holding the pinch rods together firmly, lift them out of the frame and check to see if they fit the other diagonal exactly. If the diagonals are different, slacken the clamps and set them at a slight angle to pull the frame square, then check the diagonals again.

WOODWORKING ADHESIVES

Supplied in liquid form, or as a powder or granules for mixing with water, woodworking glues can be applied with a brush, roller or spreader. All adhesives are absorbed into the wood's cell structure, forming a strong link between the fibers of both halves of a joint; however, those that set by evaporation are rarely water-resistant. For a bond in moist conditions, select one that cures by chemical reaction.

APPLYING WOODWORKING GLUE

Joints should be made to fit well, rather than relying on the gap-filling properties of adhesive. Make sure the gluing surfaces are clean and free from grease. Some woods, such as teak and rosewood, are best glued as soon after cutting as possible, before their natural resins form a surface film that prevents glue being absorbed properly.

Working in a warm, dry atmosphere, apply glue in a thin, even layer to both halves of a joint. Take care to coat the surfaces of a mortise, since most of the glue applied to the tenon is wiped off as the joint is assembled.

Don't rush when gluing up, but work as quickly as practicable, in order to assemble joints before the wood begins to swell and the glue starts to jell. For a large or complicated assembly, use a two-part glue that is applied separately to joining surfaces. Place glued components in clamps, and wipe off excess adhesive with a damp cloth.

PVA adhesive

Commonly known as white glue, polyvinyl-acetate (PVA) glue is a popular and convenient adhesive for joint-making. A ready-mixed emulsion supplied in plastic bottles, PVA sets by evaporation. It is a non-toxic glue that is easy to apply and is almost clear when set.

General-purpose PVA glue is only suitable for interior work. Although it forms a strong bond, the glue line remains relatively flexible and may creep (allow movement) when a joint is subjected to a prolonged heavy load. It does not sand well, as friction causes the glue to soften and clog abrasive paper.

Yellow aliphatic-resin PVA glue is similar to the general-purpose version, but has improved moisture resistance and is less flexible.

Chemical-bonding, 'cross-linking' PVA glue is even more water-resistant, and forms an exceptionally strong bond.

Urea- and resorcinol-resin adhesives

Urea-formaldehyde-resin glue is a two-part adhesive that sets by chemical reaction. It is an excellent water-resistant adhesive that dries with a hard glue line. The resin and hardener are usually supplied pre-mixed as dry powders that are activated when mixed with water; the mixture remains workable for 20 minutes.

With some urea glues, the resin is packaged with a separate liquid hardener. The resin is applied to one half of the joint, the hardener to the other, and the glue only begins to set when the joint is assembled.

For even greater strength coupled with superior water-resistance, choose a resorcinol-formaldehyde glue, a two-part adhesive that is mixed prior to application. Either a liquid resin is supplied with a powdered hardener; or both constituents are in liquid form. Resorcinol resin dries to a reddish-brown glue line.

When working with uncured glue that contains formaldehyde, always work in a well-ventilated workshop, and wear a face mask, gloves and eye protectors.

Hide glue

Traditional hide glue has been largely superseded by synthetic-resin adhesives, but still has advantages for furniture restoration and veneering. It is a strong-smelling, but non-toxic, glue made from animal skins and bone. It forms a strong bond that can be reversed by the application of heat and moisture. Hide glue is usually supplied in granular form for dissolving in water heated in a jacketed glue pot. When rendered to a smooth, runny consistency, the glue is applied hot to both joining surfaces. It sets, by cooling and evaporation, in about two hours.

A

abrasive paper 103
adjustable dado blades 54, 60, 96, 98, 122
adjustable fingers 84–5, 87
angled mortise 77

B

back cutting 85
backing board 44
bead 75
bevels 21, 24, 33, 39, 44, 49, 58, 82, 112
  adjustable 82
  sliding 58, 112
biscuit jointer 23–4, 120
biscuit joints 23–4, 120
bits 78, 108, 110, 119
  auger 78
  dowel 119
  drill 108, 119
  drill-and-countersink 119
  Forstner 110, 119
  screwdriver 118
blade guards 18, 24, 28, 37
blind dovetail 92
block joint 109
blocks 18, 43, 52, 60, 103
bolts 106–7, 109
bosses 108, 110
brackets 99–100
brads 20, 31, 41, 42, 106
bridle joints 35–40
butt joints 17–25, 29, 30–4, 42, 108, 114
  carcass 32
  corner 23
  edge-to-edge 26
  right-angle 33
  square-ended 18, 30

C

cabinets 21, 31, 41, 52–3, 63, 68, 74, 82, 88, 91, 105–9
cam fittings 110
canvas-stretcher joint 39
chairs 63, 69, 76, 105
chamfers 100–1, 107
chipboard fasteners 108
chisels 64–5, 76–8, 83, 90, 116
  bevel-edge 83, 86, 90, 116
  firmer 116
  hollow 78
  mortise 64–5, 116
  paring 116
  straight 76
chuck 78
clamp bars 84
clamps 124–125
  bar 26, 124–5
  C- 31, 96, 124
  fast-action 124
  handscrews 124
  miter 124

  pipe 124–5
collars 106
collets 121
compasses 100
compound miter 20
corner bridle joint 36–8, 40
corner joints 33, 41, 95
corner lap joint 59–60
corner plates 107
corner-butt joint 18, 23–4
cradles 94
cross lap joint 56–8
cupboards 33, 48, 50, 107
cutter block 78
cutters 27, 45, 48, 51, 61, 78, 84–5, 98, 102–4, 115, 121
  combination-plane 27
  concave 102
  convex 102
  cove 104, 121
  dovetail 121
  planer-thicknesser 78
  power-router 45, 61, 84–5, 98
  self-guiding 104
  straight 121
cutting gauges 42, 44, 49, 52, 53, 82–3, 90, 92–3, 100, 102–3
cutting guide 23

D

dado heads 46, 54, 60, 122
dado joints 47–54
  stopped 50
  through 48, 53
dados 47–54, 68
  stopped 50, 52, 68
  straight-sided 47
  through 47
depth gauge 69
doors 48, 66, 73
dovetail jig 87, 90
dovetail joints 16, 81–94
  half-blind 90–1
  mitered 93
  mitered through 88
  mock 94
  rabbeted through 89
  through 82–6, 89
dovetail lap joint 62
dovetail slots 94
dovetailed dado 51
dovetails 45, 47, 49, 51–2, 62, 81–2, 84–7, 91, 92–4, 98
  blind 92
  decorative 87
  decorative through 86
  half-blind 45
  half-depth 86
  mitered 93
  mitered through 88
  mock 93, 98
  secret mitered 92
  sliding 52

  through 82–6, 89
dowel bits 30, 34, 119
dowel blocks 109
dowel joints 22, 29–34
dowel rods 30, 32
dowel-reinforced miter 33
dowelled frame joint 34
dowelled miter joint 44
dowelling jig 30–3
dowels 22, 30, 33, 36, 44, 59, 106, 109–10
  coarse-threaded 110
  cranked 110
  double-ended 110
  locating 106
  metal 110
  molded 109
  stopped 44
  straight 110
drawers 23, 42, 45, 67, 81, 89, 91, 95
drill bits 30–4, 36, 78, 108, 119
drill press 34, 77, 101
drill stand 34
drills 32–4, 50, 77–8, 105, 119
  augers 78
  depth gauges 34
  depth stops 32–3
drop leaves 99–100, 102–4

E

edge stop 91
edge-to-edge joints 23, 25–8, 32, 34, 110, 114, 125
  butt 26, 32, 114

F

fences 16, 18, 20–4, 27–8, 31–4, 37, 43, 45, 51, 54, 56, 58, 60, 79, 80, 94, 96–8, 104, 120–22
  bevel 24
  end 32
  guide 104
  miter 18, 21–2, 43, 54, 56, 58, 80, 96, 98, 122
  power-router 27–8, 45, 94, 104
  radial-arm-saw 43, 60, 80
  sliding 31
  sliding-miter 96
  table-saw 20, 79, 97
files 79, 101
fine-adjustment scales 85
finger joints 15, 95–98
  mock 98
finish nails 18, 42
fixed head 31, 33
flanges 107
flat-frame miter joint 21
fluting 30
frame joints 30–1, 34
frames 17–22, 30, 35–41, 53, 55, 60–4, 70, 73–6, 105–6, 109
  box 21–2, 41

  cross 55
  flat 18, 21
  molded sections 19
  picture 17
  upholstered 106
framing 55

G

glazing-bar lap joint 57
glazing-rabbet tongue 57
glue 53, 59, 126
gouges 76–7, 101, 116
guide batten 45
guide blocks 76, 101
guide bushes 84, 87, 91

H

half-blind dovetail joint 90–2
half-blind tongue-and-rabbet 45–6
half-depth dovetail 86
half-depth pins 87
half-lap joints 55–62
hammers 117
haunches 66, 70–1, 74–6, 80
  sloping 70–1
hinge joints 99–104
hinges 99–104
  back-flap 102
  integral wooden 99
  pivoting wooden 100

I

inserts 108, 110
insulation tape 32

J

jigs 16, 19, 21, 31, 34, 37, 46, 54, 61, 77–80, 84–5, 87, 90–1, 93–4, 96, 98, 108
  corner-joint 34
  cradle 94, 98
  dovetail 87, 90
  fixed-finger dovetail 90
  right-angle 31
  tenon-cutting 37, 46, 79, 80

K

keys 108
knock-down joints 105–110
  corner 107
  edge-to-edge 110
knuckle joint 100–1

L

lap dovetail 62
lap joints 56–9
  corner 59
  cross 56–8
  glazing-bar 57
  oblique 58
leaves 99, 100, 102–4
legs 30–1, 40, 63–4, 67, 69, 71, 77, 106, 107

linings 28
lippings 48
locating strips 98
lock miter joint 46

M

mallets 117
marking gauges 112
marking knives 112
mechanical fittings 105
miter blocks 57
miter boxes 19, 57
miter clamps 19, 124
miter fences 18, 21–2, 43, 54,
  56, 58, 80, 96, 98, 122
  sliding 96, 122
miter joints 17, 19–22, 24,
  33–4, 44–5, 93, 98
  butt 17, 19–20
  dowel-reinforced 33
  flat-frame 21
  lock 46
  rabbet 44
  reinforced 22
miter shooting board 19
miter squares 19, 38–9, 44,
  58–9, 93, 112
mitered board 33
mitered bridle joint 38
mitered butt joint 19–21
mitered carcass joint 33
mitered corner bridle joint 38
mitered corners 59
mitered dovetail 93
mitered dovetail joint 93
mitered lap joint 59
mitered rabbet joint 44
mitered shoulders 39
mitered through dovetail 88
mitered-corner joint 23
miters 21–2, 38, 44, 46, 57,
  75–6, 88, 93–4, 110
  box-frame 22
  frame 21
molded joint 99
molded section 57
moldings 75, 88, 102–4
mortise and tenons 29, 63–80
  corner 77
  double 66
  grooved-frame 74
  haunched 70–1, 74, 76
  loose-wedged 73
  molded-frame 76
  rabbeted-frame 75
  through 64–5
  twin 67–8
  wedged 72–3
mortise-and-tenon joints
  35–6, 40, 63–80
mortise gauges 20, 36, 38–40,
  64, 67, 74, 75, 77
mortises 36–8, 40, 63–80
  open 37–8

stopped 74, 78
  through 68, 78
mortising attachments 78
mortising table 78
mountings 97

N

nail sets 42, 117
nuts 106–7

O

oblique lap joint 58
open mortise and tenon 39

P

packing strip 97
picture-frame joint 19
pilot hole 107
pin shoulder line 86
pin tenons 67–8
pinch rod 125
pinned mortise and tenon 68
pins 82–90, 92–3
  half-depth 87
  triangular 86
planer-thicknesser 78
planes 114–5
  bench 18–9, 26, 114
  block 19, 38, 115
  bull-nose 115
  combination 27, 115
  jack 114
  plow 27, 115
  rabbet 103, 114
  router 48–50, 52, 115
  shoulder 38, 42, 44, 53, 92–3,
  101, 115
  smoothing 114
  try 26, 114
polish 18
power routers 121
  ball-bearing guide 104
  base 61
  collet 121
  cove cutter 104
  cross-bar attachments 87
  cutters 45, 61, 84–5, 94, 98
  depth stop 78
  fences 27–8, 45, 51, 94
  guide fence 104
  hold-down guard 28
  tables 51, 79, 94
push stick 16
putty 75

R

rabbet joints 41–6
  mitered 44
rabbet shoulders 53–4
rabbeted through dovetail 88
rabbets 28, 41–6, 53, 74, 76,
  88, 102–3, 114
radial-arm saws 123
  end stops 43, 60, 80

fences 43, 60, 80, 123
  table 97
rails 30–1, 34, 40, 63–4, 66–7,
  69–76, 100, 106–7
  lock 66
reinforced miter joint 19
right-angle corner 55
rubbed joints 26, 125
rule joint 102–4

S

saw fence 22
saws 113, 122
  back 52
  coping 40, 66–8, 83, 86–7,
  101, 113
  dovetail 82–3, 86–90, 92, 113
  fine-tooth 30
  miter 19
  plunge 23
  radial-arm 20, 22, 43, 46,
  60–1, 80, 97, 122
  table 18, 20, 28, 37, 43, 45–6,
  54, 56, 58, 61, 79, 96–8, 122
  tenon 40, 42, 48, 50–1, 59,
  62, 68, 113
scratch stock 102–3
screw fittings 108
screw slot 106
screw socket 109
screwdrivers 105, 109–10, 118
secret mitered dovetail 93
self-assembly furniture 105
shelves 47–52, 68, 109
shooting board 18
shoulder lines 14, 42, 44
shoulders 18, 19, 31, 33, 36–40,
  42–3, 48–52, 56–62, 64–70,
  72–7, 80–90, 92–3, 101, 107
  angled 59
  glazing-rabbet 57
  side 31, 33
  sloping 19
  square 39–40
  tapered 52
side panel 50
side stop 84
slide 80
slide rod 33
sliding crosscut table 18
sliding dovetail 52
slot mortiser 78
slots 63, 96
slotting jig 21
socket block 109
sockets 85, 87, 108–9
  hexagonal 108
  pin-and-tail 85
spacers 37, 43, 46, 54
spanners 107
spindle molder 96
splines 20, 27–8, 93, 94, 98
splitter 28
square-cut joint 17

square-shoulder joint 62
stile molding 76
stiles 30–1, 34, 63–5, 69–71, 73–6
stocks 36, 38–40, 44, 67
stopped dado joint 50
stopped mortise-and-tenon 69
stopped pins 68
stopped tenons 72
stopper 20
straight sliding dovetail 49–50
straightedge 112
stretchers 39
stud partitioning 17

T

T-bridle joint 40
T-butt joint 23
T-joints 23–4, 33, 55
T-lap joint 60–2
T-square 51
table saws 122
  blade guards 18, 28, 37
  end stops 79
  fences 20, 79, 97, 122
  rip fences 28, 37, 43, 46, 54,
  56, 80
tables 40, 63, 69, 76, 99–107
tails 81–90, 92
tape 32, 69
tape measure 14, 112
tapers 82
templates 54, 62, 64, 66, 68, 70,
  74, 82, 84–93, 102, 112
  dovetail 82, 86, 92, 93, 112
  finger 91
tenons 35–8, 40, 63–80
  barefaced 77
  skewed 77
through dado joint 48, 53
through dovetail joint 82–6, 89
through dovetails 15, 82–6, 89
through joints 64–6, 86, 89
through tenons 15, 69, 72
tongue and groove 25, 41
tongue-and-groove joint 27–8
tongue-and-rabbet joint 45,
  53–4
tongues 20–2, 27–8, 45–6,
  53–7, 63, 70, 96, 97
try square 112

U

underframe 40

V

veneer 22
vertical dividers 109

W

washers 106
wax 18, 20
wedges 39, 64, 68, 72–3
  fox 72
  loose 73